Hands-On Design Patterns with React Native

Proven techniques and patterns for efficient native mobile development with JavaScript

Mateusz Grzesiukiewicz

BIRMINGHAM - MUMBAI

Hands-On Design Patterns with React Native

Commissioning Editor: Amarabha Banerjee
Acquisition Editor: Devanshi Doshi
Content Development Editor: Aishwarya Gawankar
Technical Editor: Leena Patil
Copy Editor: Safis Editing
Project Coordinator: Sheejal Shah
Proofreader: Safis Editing
Indexer: Tejal Daruwale Soni
Graphics: Alishon Mendonsa
Production Coordinator: Nilesh Mohite

First edition: September 2018

Production reference: 1280918

Published by Packt Publishing Ltd.
Livery Place
35 Livery Street
Birmingham
B3 2PB, UK.

ISBN 978-1-78899-446-0

www.packtpub.com

To all the people who create interfaces that save our lives.

– Mateusz Grzesiukiewicz

`mapt.io`

Mapt is an online digital library that gives you full access to over 5,000 books and videos, as well as industry leading tools to help you plan your personal development and advance your career. For more information, please visit our website.

Why subscribe?

- Spend less time learning and more time coding with practical eBooks and Videos from over 4,000 industry professionals

- Improve your learning with Skill Plans built especially for you

- Get a free eBook or video every month

- Mapt is fully searchable

- Copy and paste, print, and bookmark content

Packt.com

Did you know that Packt offers eBook versions of every book published, with PDF and ePub files available? You can upgrade to the eBook version at `www.packt.com` and as a print book customer, you are entitled to a discount on the eBook copy. Get in touch with us at `customercare@packt.com` for more details.

At `www.packt.com`, you can also read a collection of free technical articles, sign up for a range of free newsletters, and receive exclusive discounts and offers on Packt books and eBooks.

Contributors

About the author

Mateusz Grzesiukiewicz has worked on numerous big projects, including an investment banking platform at Goldman Sachs, a Jira project management tool at Atlassian, and a recruitment portal at GoldenLine. Every of these projects served millions of people, which made them great opportunities to test scalability and the industry's best design patterns. He strives to popularize the common patterns and help people grow their technology at scale. He has spent hundreds of hours teaching, for instance at a private programming school called Coder's Lab. He has over 5,000 students registered on his online React course on Udemy. He would love to bring programming to every household, hence this book—*Hands-On Design Patterns with React Native*.

Big thanks to all of the great editors who spent hours reading my silly drafts. To all of the people who kept me mentally safe while I worked 16 hours a day to deliver the quality this topic deserved. Bows to my family, who created warm and welcoming vibrations, especially those who will never understand a word of this book. To Jolanta and Dariusz, my parents.

About the reviewer

Tiago Guizelini is a senior full-stack developer from São Paulo, Brazil. He loves developing mobile apps using Android and React Native, building REST APIs with Java or Node.js, and frontend development with React.js and Angular.

> *I would like to thank my wife, Dayane, for supporting my work and understanding me as a person I am.*

Packt is searching for authors like you

If you're interested in becoming an author for Packt, please visit `authors.packtpub.com` and apply today. We have worked with thousands of developers and tech professionals, just like you, to help them share their insight with the global tech community. You can make a general application, apply for a specific hot topic that we are recruiting an author for, or submit your own idea.

Table of Contents

Preface

Frameworks and libraries come and go. Design patterns usually stay for longer. In this book, we do a mix of learning React Native and design patterns relevant to this ecosystem. When it comes to React, the essential knowledge about design patterns is spread all over the place. Sometimes it's buried in proprietary code bases. This book brings it to you. I call them **idea patterns:** hands-on design patterns that are explained with real working examples. In this book we use React Native, but you can successfully use most of those patterns in web development with React, or even other frameworks, such as Angular or Vue. Hopefully you will use this knowledge to build well thought-out and easy-to-maintain code bases. Good luck with this endeavor!

Who this book is for

Amateur programmers and passionate people are very welcome to read this book, but expect that it may be more challenging than elementary programming books.

I assume you have some programming experience in JavaScript and that the terminal window is not foreign to you. Ideally, you should work as a developer (junior/mid/senior) so you will have a broad perspective and can immediately apply the knowledge to your work. Experience in developing mobile applications is not required.

What this book covers

Chapter 1, *React Component Patterns*, is the starting point of our journey. We need to understand the core building blocks of our application: React components. You will learn how to properly use presentational and container components.

Chapter 2, *View Patterns*, will dive into the best approaches into writing view code. You will learn the patterns that decouple view layer from the rest of the app. Also, in this chapter we learn about the basics of React Native: its most important components that are available out of the box. For the first time, our application code will be automatically tested by tooling such as Linter.

Chapter 3, *Styling Patterns*, is a chapter dedicated to design patterns built around styling. You get a look at the patterns that mobile designers need to follow. On top of that, we will learn Flexbox pattern and learn how to properly create and measure animations in React Native.

Chapter 4, *Flux Architecture*, finally looks at the architecture. Flux will enable us to scale our frontend code much more easily. For the first time, we will introduce Dispatcher and Stores into our application.

Chapter 5, *Store Patterns*, focuses on one important part of Flux: Store. You will learn about the Redux and Mobx state management libraries. By the end of the chapter, you will know how to make Store your application's single source of truth.

Chapter 6, *Data Transfer Patterns*, walks you through patterns that involve so-called side effects. We will use the local server and the API that our React Native code will consume. You will learn how to decouple such processes from the main application code using Redux Thunk and Redux Saga libraries

Chapter 7, *Navigation Patterns*, shows you the difficult part of the mobile application: navigation. We will dive into cross-platform problems and see how to handle them using either React Navigation or React Native Navigation.

Chapter 8, *JavaScript and ECMAScript Patterns*, starts with the JavaScript iterator pattern and then walks you through useful functions within JavaScript, ECMAScript, and in a Ramda library. After all that, we discuss some of the functional approaches that are related to the next chapter.

Chapter 9, *Elements of Functional Programming Patterns*, explores the unique world of Functional Programming patterns. Some of them are really famous in React and React Native applications. This chapter aims to explain why and helps you make a right decision if you should take more Functional Programming techniques into your project.

Chapter 10, *Managing Dependencies*, draws your attention to dependency injection, and how to avoid usage of Singleton pattern. You will learn about the React context API and see how libraries have been leveraging dependency injection in the past.

Chapter 11, *Type Checking Patterns*, teaches you how to type your application. We will do a walk-through of TypeScript's capabilities. By the end, you will be able to type the whole application. You will learn what nominal and structural typing are.

To get the most out of this book

Take your time, don't rush. You don't need to read this book in a week.

Come back to this book as your developer career progresses. You will focus on completely different things, and this way you will learn the most out of this book.

Play with the examples I have prepared. Each is a standalone application so you can play and improve the code as we go. This is meant to serve as a playground so you can not only learn from the examples but create extensions of them. As you build, you will understand the changes that are introduced section after section. If you just read the book, you will definitely miss this perspective.

Download the example code files

You can download the example code files for this book from your account at `www.packt.com`. If you purchased this book elsewhere, you can visit `www.packt.com/support` and register to have the files emailed directly to you.

You can download the code files by following these steps:

1. Log in or register at `www.packt.com`.
2. Select the **SUPPORT** tab.
3. Click on **Code Downloads & Errata**.
4. Enter the name of the book in the **Search** box and follow the onscreen instructions.

Once the file is downloaded, please make sure that you unzip or extract the folder using the latest version of:

- WinRAR/7-Zip for Windows
- Zipeg/iZip/UnRarX for Mac
- 7-Zip/PeaZip for Linux

The code bundle for the book is also hosted on GitHub at `https://github.com/Ajdija/hands-on-design-patterns-with-react-native`. In case there's an update to the code, it will be updated on the existing GitHub repository.

We also have other code bundles from our rich catalog of books and videos available at `https://github.com/PacktPublishing/`. Check them out!

Download the color images

We also provide a PDF file that has color images of the screenshots/diagrams used in this book. You can download it here: `https://www.packtpub.com/sites/default/files/downloads/9781788994460_ColorImages.pdf`.

Conventions used

There are a number of text conventions used throughout this book.

`CodeInText`: Indicates code words in text, database table names, folder names, filenames, file extensions, pathnames, dummy URLs, user input, and Twitter handles. Here is an example: "Mount the downloaded `WebStorm-10*.dmg` disk image file as another disk in your system."

A block of code is set as follows:

```
export default function() {
    return React.createElement(
        Text,
        {style: {marginTop: 30}},
        'Example Text!'
    );
}
```

When we wish to draw your attention to a particular part of a code block, the relevant lines or items are set in bold:

```
export default function App() {
  return (
      <View style={styles.container}>
        ...
      </View>
  );
}
```

Any command-line input or output is written as follows:

```
yarn test -- --coverage
```

Bold: Indicates a new term, an important word, or words that you see onscreen. For example, words in menus or dialog boxes appear in the text like this. Here is an example: "You can now tap the **Details** button to navigate to the Task Details screen."

Warnings or important notes appear like this.

 Tips and tricks appear like this.

Get in touch

Feedback from our readers is always welcome.

General feedback: If you have questions about any aspect of this book, mention the book title in the subject of your message and email us at customercare@packtpub.com.

Errata: Although we have taken every care to ensure the accuracy of our content, mistakes do happen. If you have found a mistake in this book, we would be grateful if you would report this to us. Please visit www.packt.com/submit-errata, selecting your book, clicking on the Errata Submission Form link, and entering the details.

Piracy: If you come across any illegal copies of our works in any form on the Internet, we would be grateful if you would provide us with the location address or website name. Please contact us at copyright@packt.com with a link to the material.

If you are interested in becoming an author: If there is a topic that you have expertise in and you are interested in either writing or contributing to a book, please visit authors.packtpub.com.

Reviews

Please leave a review. Once you have read and used this book, why not leave a review on the site that you purchased it from? Potential readers can then see and use your unbiased opinion to make purchase decisions, we at Packt can understand what you think about our products, and our authors can see your feedback on their book. Thank you!

For more information about Packt, please visit packt.com.

React Component Patterns

Developing Android and iOS has never been easier than it is now. React Native has changed how fast we develop new apps and deliver value to the end user. Knowing this technology will give you a great edge in the market. I'm Matt and I'm happy to show you the best practices I have learned while working in a React Native ecosystem. Through this book, we will explore design patterns by example. In just this first chapter, we will create over 10 small applications. Later on in this book, we will create more complex applications, using the patterns that I will gradually introduce to you.

In this chapter, we will explore React patterns that also apply to the React Native world. The most crucial patterns you need to understand are stateless and stateful components. Understanding how to use these will make you a much better React Native developer and empower you with standard patterns in every React Native application.

When it comes to components, it is crucial to make them as reusable as possible and follow the well-known programmer principle—**Don't Repeat Yourself (DRY)**. Presentational components and container components are meant to do just that. We will dive into them with a couple of examples to learn how to split features into reusable pieces.

To be more precise, in this first chapter, we will look at the following topics:

- Stateless and stateful components, using short and then more complex examples
- How to create reusable and easily configurable presentational components
- Container components and their role in the encapsulation of features
- When to compose components and how to create **Higher Order Components (HOCs)**

It's time to act on your side. **Prepare your environment for React Native development right now** if you want to follow along and play with the examples. Most of the code samples that you will see in this book can be run and displayed either on a simulator or on a real mobile device. Now, make sure that you can launch the Hello World example on your mobile or simulator.

Code examples are checked into a Git repository on GitHub, which can be found at https://github.com/Ajdija/hands-on-design-patterns-with-react-native.
Please follow the readme.md instructions to set up your machine and launch our first example. The Hello World example can be found in the following directory src/Chapter_1_React_component_patterns/Example_1_Hello_World.

Stateless and stateful components

First of all, let's look at the first stateless component that has been created for us. It has been automatically generated by **Create React Native App (CRNA)** for our Hello World application. This component was created using the class syntax that was introduced in ECMAScript 2015 (ES6). Such components are usually called **class components**:

```
// src/ Chapter 1/ Example 1_Hello World/ App.js

export default class App extends React.Component {
  render() {
    return (
      <View style={styles.container}>
        <Text>Hands-On Design Patterns with React Native</Text>
        <Text>Chapter 1: React Component Patterns</Text>
        <Text style={styles.text}>You are ready to start the journey.
        Fun fact is, this text is rendered by class component called
        App. Check App.js if you want to look it up.</Text>
      </View>
    );
  }
}
```

Class components can be used to create stateful components.

 The code samples provided in this book use ECMAScript 2018 syntax with Stage 3 feature *class field declarations*. Babel is the transpiler that supports such code by relevant plugins that are pre-configured for us by the CRNA toolbox. If you decide not to use CRNA, then you may need to configure Babel yourself.

However, in this case, the class component is unnecessary. We can safely use a stateless one, as it's simpler. Let's see how we can declare a **stateless component**. The most common approach is by using ES6 arrow syntax. Such components are called **functional components**. Check out the following code to see what our rewritten component looks like:

```
const App = () => (
    <View style={styles.container}>
      <Text>Hands-On Design Patterns with React Native</Text>
      <Text>Chapter 1: React Component Patterns</Text>
      <Text style={styles.text}>You are ready to start the journey. Fun
      fact is, this text is rendered by Functional Component called
      App. Check App.js if you want to look it up.</Text>
    </View>
);
export default App;
```

If you are not a fan of arrow syntax, you can also use regular `function` syntax:

```
// src/ Chapter 1/ Example_2_Functional_Components/ App.js

export default function App() {
  return (
      <View style={styles.container}>
          ...
      </View>
  );
}
```

The very first question that pop ups is: why is it stateless? The answer is simple: it doesn't contain any inner state. This means that we are not storing any private data inside it. Everything the component needs to render itself is provided from the external world, which the component does not care about.

In this little example, we actually never pass any external data to the component. Let's do that now. To do so, we will create another component called `HelloText` that consumes one property: text to display. The usual convention to pass the text to such a component is to place the text between the opening and closing tag, for instance, `<HelloText> example text that is passed </HelloText>`. Hence, to retrieve such a prop within our functional component, we will need to use a special key called `children`:

```
// src/ Chapter 1/ Example_3_Functional_Components_with_props/ App.js

const HelloText = ({children, ...otherProps}) => (
    <Text {...otherProps}>{children}</Text>
);
const App = () => (
    <View style={styles.container}>
        <HelloText>
            Hands-On Design Patterns with React Native
        </HelloText>
        <HelloText>Chapter 1: React Component Patterns</HelloText>
        <HelloText style={styles.text}>
            You are ready to start the journey. Fun fact is, this text
            is rendered by Functional Component called HelloText.
            Check App.js if you want to look it up.
        </HelloText>
    </View>
);
export default App;
```

Using the `children` prop makes our `HelloText` component way more powerful. Props are a very flexible mechanism. Using props, you can send any valid JavaScript type. In this case, we have sent just text, but you can send other components, too.

It's time to add some vitality to our component. We will make it expand the third text block, but only after pressing the chapter or title text. For this functionality, we need to store a state that remembers if the component is expanded or collapsed.

Here is what you need to do:

1. Change the component to the class syntax.
2. Leverage the state object of the React library. We must initialize the state within the class constructor and make the text collapsed by default.
3. Add conditional rendering to the component `render` function.
4. Add the press handler, which will change the state once we tap on the title or chapter text.

The solution is presented in the following code:

```
// src/ Chapter 1/ Example_4_Stateful_expandable_component/ App.js

export default class App extends React.Component {
    constructor() {
        super();
        this.state = {
            // default state on first render
            expanded: false
        }
    }

    expandOrCollapse() {
        // toggle expanded: true becomes false, false becomes true
        this.setState({expanded: !this.state.expanded});
    }

    render = () => (
        <View style={styles.container}>
            <HelloText onPress={() => this.expandOrCollapse()}>
                Hands-On Design Patterns with React Native
            </HelloText>
            <HelloText onPress={() => this.expandOrCollapse()}>
                Chapter 1: React Component Patterns
            </HelloText>
            {
                this.state.expanded &&
                <HelloText style={styles.text}>
                    You can expand and collapse this text by clicking
                    the Title or Chapter text. Bonus: Check Chapter 4
                    to learn how to animate expanding andcollapsing.
                </HelloText>
            }
        </View>
    );
}
```

Congratulations—we have made our first stateless and stateful components!

Note the && operator that displays the component. If a Boolean value on the left side of the operator is true, then the component on the right-hand side will be displayed. The whole expression needs to be wrapped into curly brackets. We will explore more of its capabilities in Chapter 3, *Style Patterns*.

It's time to create something more challenging: `Task list`. Please start over and prepare your code. Clean up `App.js` so that it only includes the `App` class component:

1. The constructor should initialize the task list in its state. In my example, the task list will be an array of strings.
2. Iterate over the tasks to create the `Text` component for each task. This should happen in the `render` function of the `App` component. Please note that you can simplify iteration by using the `map` function instead of a regular `for` loop. Doing this should become second nature, since it's became a standard in almost every JS project.

My solution is presented in the following code:

```js
// src/ Chapter 1/ Example 5_Task_list/ App.js

export default class App extends React.Component {
  constructor() {
    super();
    // Set the initial state, tasks is an array of strings
    this.state = {
      tasks: ['123', '456']
    }
  }

  render = () => (
      <View style={styles.container}>
        {
          this.state.tasks
          .map((task, index) => (
              <Text key={index} style={styles.text}>{task}</Text>
          ))
        }
      </View>
  );
}
```

Iterating using `map` is a nice feature, but the whole component doesn't look like a task list yet. Don't worry, you will learn how to style components in `Chapter 3`, *Style Patterns*.

What are the advantages of stateless components?

It may seem tempting to only use stateful class components and develop a whole application like that. Why would we even bother with stateless functional components? The answer is performance. Stateless functional components can be rendered faster. One of the reasons why this is the case is because stateless functional components do not require some of the life cycle hooks.

 What are life cycle hooks? React components have life cycles. This means that they have different stages like mounting, unmounting, and updating. You can hook each stage and even sub stage. Please check the official React documentation to see the full list of available life cycle methods: `https://reactjs.org/docs/state-and-lifecycle.html`. These are useful to trigger fetching data from the API or to update the view.

Please note that if you are using React v16 or later, it is not true that functional components are wrapped into class components internally within the React library:

"Functional components in React 16 don't go through the same code path as class components, unlike in the previous version where they were converted to classes and would have the same code path. Class components have additional checks that are required and overhead in creating the instances that simple functions don't have. These are micro-optimizations though and shouldn't make a huge difference in real-world apps – unless your class component is overly complex."

- Dominic Gannaway, engineer on the React core team at Facebook (`https://github.com/reactjs/reactjs.org/issues/639#issuecomment-367858928`)

Functional components are faster, but in most cases are outperformed by class components extending `React.PureComponent`:

"Still, to be clear, they don't bail out of rendering like PureComponent does when props are shallowly equal."

- Dan Abramov, co-author of Redux and Create React App, engineer on the React core team at Facebook (`https://twitter.com/trueadm/status/916706152976707584`)

Functional components are not only more concise, but they usually are also pure functions. We will explore this concept further in Chapter 9, *Elements of Functional Programming Patterns*. Pure functions provide a lot of benefits, such as a predictable UI and easy tracking of user behavior. The application can be implemented in a certain way to record user actions. Such data helps with debugging and reproducing errors in tests. We will dig into this topic later on in this book.

Component composition

If you have learned any **Object-Oriented (OO)** language, you may have used inheritance extensively. In JavaScript, this concept is a little bit different. JavaScript inheritance is based on prototypes, and so we call it **prototypal inheritance**. Functionalities are not copied to the object itself—they are inherited from the prototype of the object and possibly even through other prototypes in the prototype tree. We call this a **prototype chain**.

However, in React, using inheritance is not very common. Thanks to components, we can embrace another pattern called **component composition**. Instead of creating a new class and inheriting from the base class, we will create a new parent component that will use its child component to make itself more specific or more powerful. Let's look at an example:

```
// src/ Chapter 1/ Example_6_Component_composition_red_text/ App.js

const WarningText = ({style, ...otherProps}) => (
    <Text style={[style, {color: 'orange'}]} {...otherProps} />
);

export default class App extends React.Component {
    render = () => (
        <View style={styles.container}>
            <Text style={styles.text}>Normal text</Text>
            <WarningText style={styles.text}>Warning</WarningText>
        </View>
    );
}
```

The App component is being built out of three components: View, Text, and WarningText. It is a perfect example of how one component, through composition, can reuse the capabilities of others.

The WarningText component uses composition to enforce the orange text color in the Text component. It makes the generic Text component more specific. Now, we can reuse WarningText in any place of the app where it is necessary. If our app designer decides to alter the warning text, we can quickly adapt to the new design in one place.

Note the implicit pass of a special prop called children. It represents the children of the component. In `Example 6_ Component composition – red text`, we first pass warning text as children to the `WarningText` component and then using the spread operator it is passed to the `Text` component, which `WarningText` encapsulates.

Composing the application layout

Let's suppose we have to create a welcome screen for our application. It should be divided into three sections—header, main content, and footer. We would like to have consistent margins and styling for both logged and anonymous users. However, the header and footer content will differ. Our next task is to create a component that supports these requirements.

Let's create a welcome screen that will use a generic component for encapsulating an app layout.

Follow this step-by-step guide to do so:

1. Create the `AppLayout` component that enforces some styling. It should accept three props: `header`, `MainContent`, and `Footer`:

```
const AppLayout = ({Header, MainContent, Footer}) => (
    // These three props can be any component that we pass.
    // You can think of it as a function that
    // can accept any kind of parameter passed to it.
    <View style={styles.container}>
        <View style={styles.layoutHeader}>{Header}</View>
        <View style={styles.layoutContent}>{MainContent}</View>
        <View style={styles.layoutFooter}>{Footer}</View>
    </View>
);
```

2. It's now time to create placeholders for header, footer, and content. We have created three components: `WelcomeHeader`, `WelcomeContent`, and `WelcomeFooter`. If you wish, you can extend them to be more complex than a trivial piece of text:

```
const WelcomeHeader = () => <View><Text>Header</Text></View>;
const WelcomeContent = () => <View><Text>Content</Text></View>;
const WelcomeFooter = () => <View><Text>Footer</Text></View>;
```

3. We should connect `AppLayout` with our placeholder components. Create the `WelcomeScreen` component, which will pass placeholder components (from *step 2*) down to the `AppLayout` as props:

```
const WelcomeScreen = () => (
    <AppLayout
        Header={<WelcomeHeader />}
        MainContent={<WelcomeContent />}
        Footer={<WelcomeFooter />}
    />
);
```

4. The last step is going to be creating the root component for our app and adding some styles:

```
// src/ Chapter 1/ Example_7_App_layout_and_Welcome_screen/ App.js

// root component
export default class App extends React.Component {
    render = () => <WelcomeScreen />;
}

// styles
const styles = StyleSheet.create({
    container: {
        flex: 1,
        marginTop: 20
    },
    layoutHeader: {
        width: '100%',
        height: 100,
        backgroundColor: 'powderblue'
    },
    layoutContent: {
        flex: 1,
        width: '100%',
        backgroundColor: 'skyblue'
    },
    layoutFooter: {
        width: '100%',
        height: 100,
        backgroundColor: 'steelblue'
    }
});
```

Please note the use of `StyleSheet.create({...})`. This creates a style object that represents our app styles. In this case, we have created four different styles (`container`, `layoutHeader`, `layoutContent`, and `layoutFooter`) that will be available to use with the markup we defined. We previously customized styles using keys such as `width`, `height`, and `backgroundColor`, which are trivial. In this example, however, we also use `flex`, which comes from the term **flexbox pattern**. We will explain this approach in detail in `Chapter 3`, *Style Patterns*, where we focus primarily on `StyleSheet` patterns.

This is pretty good. We have made a trivial layout for our application and then created the welcome screen with it.

What about component inheritance?

> *"At Facebook, we use React in thousands of components, and we haven't found any use cases where we would recommend creating component inheritance hierarchies."*
> *- React official documentation* (`https://reactjs.org/docs/composition-vs-inheritance.html`)

I have not come across a situation where I had to step away from component composition in favor of inheritance. Neither have developers at Facebook (as per the preceding quotation). Hence, I highly recommend you get used to composition.

Testing components on high-level patterns

Testing is something very important when it comes to creating reliable and stable applications. First of all, let's look at the most common three types of tests you will need to write:

- **Trivial unit tests**: I don't understand it, but is it working or not working at all? Usually, tests that check whether the component renders or whether the function runs with no errors are called trivial unit tests. If you do this manually, you call these tests smoke tests. Such tests are vital to have. Whether you like it or not, you should write trivial tests, at least to know if every feature is *somehow* working.

- **Unit tests**: Does the code work as I expect it to? Does it work in all of the code branches? By branch, we mean places in the code where it branches, for instance, if statements are branching code into different code paths, which is similar to switch-case statements. Unit testing refers to testing a single unit of code. In crucial features of an application, unit tests should cover whole function code (as a principle: 100% code coverage for crucial features).

- **Snapshot tests**: Testing if the previous and actual version produce the same result is called snapshot testing. Snapshot tests are just creating text output, but once the output is proven to be correct (through developer assessment and code review), it may work as a comparison tool. Try to use snapshot tests a lot. Such tests should be committed into your repository and undergo review process. This new feature in Jest saves a lot of time for developers:

    - **Image snapshot tests:** In Jest, snapshot tests compare text (JSON to JSON), however, you may encounter references to snapshot tests on mobile devices, where this means comparing images to images. This is a more advanced topic, but is commonly used by big websites. Taking such a screenshot most likely requires building the whole app instead of a single component. Building the whole app is time-consuming, so some companies only run these type of tests when they plan for a release, for instance, on a release candidate build. This strategy can be automated to follow *continuous integration* and *continuous delivery* principles.

Since we are using the CRNA toolbox in this book, the testing solution you want to check is Jest (`https://facebook.github.io/jest/`).

Watch out if you come from a React web development background. React Native, as the name suggests, operates in a native environment and hence has many components, such as react-native-video package, which may need special testing solutions. In many cases, you will need to mock (create placeholders/mimic behaviour) these packages.
Check out `https://facebook.github.io/jest/docs/en/tutorial-react-native.html#mock-native-modules-using-jestmock` for more information.
We will address some of these concerns in Chapter 10, *Managing Dependencies*.

There are usually some metrics to testing, such as code coverage (the number of lines covered by tests), the number of reported bugs, and the number of registered errors.

Although very valuable, these may create a false belief that the application is well-tested.

There are a few utterly wrong practices that I need to mention when it comes to testing patterns:

- **Relying only on unit tests**: Unit tests mean testing just a single piece of code in isolation, for instance, a function by passing arguments to it and checking the output. This is great and saves you from a lot of bugs, but no matter what code coverage you have, you may bump into problems with the integration of well-tested components. The real-life example I like to use is a video of two sliding doors that are placed too close to each other, which causes them to keep on opening and closing forever.

- **Relying on code coverage too much**: Stop stressing yourself or other developers to reach that 100% or 90% code coverage mark. If you can afford it, great, but usually it makes developers write less valuable tests. Sometimes, it is crucial to send different integer values to functions; for instance, when testing division, it is not enough to send two positive integers. You need to also check what happens when you divide by zero. Coverage won't tell you that.

- **Not tracking how your testing metrics influence the number of bugs**: If you just rely on some metrics, whether it be code coverage or any other, please reassess if the metrics tell the truth, for instance, whether increase in the metric causes less bugs. To give you a nice example, I've heard developers from many different companies say that the code coverage increasing above 80% didn't help them much.

 If you are a product owner and have checked the point *Not tracking how your testing metrics influence the number of bugs* above, please also consult with the tech leader or senior developers of your project. There may be certain specifics that influence this process, for instance, development schedule shifting to more repeatable code. Please don't jump to conclusions too quickly.

Snapshot testing expandable components

This time, we will demonstrate a tricky part of snapshot testing.

Let's start by creating our first snapshot test. Go to `Chapter_1/Example 4_Stateful_expandable_component` and run `yarn test` in the command line. You should see that one test passes. What kind of test is it? It's a trivial unit test that's located in the `App.test.js` file.

It's time to create our first snapshot test. Replace `expect(rendered).toBeTruthy();` with `expect(rendered).toMatchSnapshot();`. It should look like this:

```
it('renders', () => {
  const rendered = renderer.create(<App />).toJSON();
  expect(rendered).toMatchSnapshot();
});
```

Once you have this, rerun `yarn test`. A new directory called `__snapshots__` should be created with the `App.test.js.snap` file inside it. Take a look at its contents. This is your first snapshot.

It's time to test the app's coverage. You can do this with the following command:

```
yarn test -- --coverage
```

It yields something a little concerning:

File	% Stmts	% Branch	% Funcs	% Lines	Uncovered Line #s
All files	66.67	50	50	66.67	
App.js	66.67	50	50	66.67	18,23,26

We have one component that has one branch (`if`), and after performing a snapshot test, the coverage is not even near 100%. What's wrong?

There is obviously a problem with the branch that relies on state, but would it account for over 30% of the lines? Let's see the full report. Open the `./coverage/lcov-report/App.js.html` file:

```
16        expandOrCollapse() {
17            // toggle expanded: true becomes false, false becomes true
18            this.setState({expanded: !this.state.expanded});
19        }
20
21        render = () => (
22  1x        <View style={styles.container}>
23            <HelloText onPress={() => this.expandOrCollapse()}>
24                Hands-On Design Patterns with React Native
25            </HelloText>
26            <HelloText onPress={() => this.expandOrCollapse()}>
27                Chapter 1: React Component Patterns
28            </HelloText>
```

The coverage report file. You can see that the code has been uncovered with the tests marked in red.

Now, you see what is wrong. The answer is pretty simple—snapshot tests do not test prop functions. Why? First of all, this does not make much sense. Why would we convert a function to JSON, and how would it help? Secondly, tell me how to serialize the function. Shall I return function code as text or compute output in some other way?

Take this example as a lesson that **snapshot tests are not enough**.

Test-driven development approach

You will often hear about the **test-driven development** (**TDD**) approach, which basically means writing tests first. To simplify this, let's summarize this in the following three steps:

1. Write tests and watch them fail.
2. Implement functionality until you see your tests passing.
3. Refactor to the best practices (optional).

I must admit that I really love this approach. However, the truth is that most developers will glorify this approach and barely any will use it. This is usually because it's time-consuming and it is hard to predict what the thing you are about to test looks like.

Going further, you will find that one of the test types is against TDD. Snapshot tests can only be created if the component is implemented, as they rely on its structure. This is another reason why snapshot tests are more of an addition to your tests rather than a replacement.

This approach works best in huge applications that go on for years, where a team of tech architects plan the interfaces and patterns to be used. This is most likely in backend projects, and you will have a general idea of how all of the classes and patterns connect to each other. Then, you simply take the interface and write the tests. Next, you follow up with implementation. If you want to create interfaces in React Native, you will need to support TypeScript.

Some argue that TDD is great in small projects, and you may quickly find such threads on Stack Overflow. Don't get me wrong; I'm happy that some people are happy. However, small projects tend to be very unstable and are likely to change often. If you are building a **Minimum Viable Product (MVP)**, it doesn't work very well with TDD. You are better off relying on the fact that the libraries you use are well-tested and deliver the project on time, while quickly testing it with snapshots.

To summarize: abandoning TDD should not mean writing less tests.

Presentational components

It's time to learn how to make components reusable. For this goal, we will use the best tool in our hands: the **presentational component** pattern. It decouples components from logic and makes them flexible.

> The presentational component is a pattern name that you will hear very often, if, later on, you decide to use the Redux library. For instance, presentational components are heavily used in Dan Abramov's Redux course.

I like to explain that the presentational component pattern is a website's world. For a long time now, there has been three leading blocks for every website: CSS, HTML, and JavaScript. React, however, introduced a bit of a different approach, that is, the automated generation of HTML based on JavaScript. HTML became virtual. Hence, you may have heard of the **Virtual Document Object Model** (**Virtual DOM**). This separation of concerns—HTML (view), CSS (styles), and JavaScript (logic, sometimes called the controller)—should remain untouched in our JavaScript-only world. Therefore, use presentational components to mimic HTML and container components for logic.

Approach this problem in the same fashion in React Native applications. The markup you write should be separated from the logic it consumes.

Let's see this in action. Do you remember Example 4_Stateful expandable component? It has one presentational component already:

```
const HelloText = ({children, ...otherProps}) => (
    <Text {...otherProps}>{children}</Text>
);
```

This component does not introduce any logic and contains only markup, which is very short in this case. Any logic that can be useful is hidden within props and passed along, as this component does not need to consume it. In more complex examples, you may need to destructure props to pass them to the right components; for example, when using the spread operator above, all props that are not destructured are being passed.

But, instead of focusing on this simple example, let's start refactoring the App component. First of all, we will move the markup to the separate presentational component:

```
// src/ Chapter_1_React_component_patterns/
// Example_9_Refactoring_to_presentational_component/ App.js
// Text has been replaced with "..." to save space.

export const HelloBox = ({ isExpanded, expandOrCollapse }) => (
    <View style={styles.container}>
        <HelloText onPress={() => expandOrCollapse()}>...</HelloText>
        <HelloText onPress={() => expandOrCollapse()}>...</HelloText>
        {
            isExpanded &&
            <HelloText style={styles.text}>...</HelloText>
        }
    </View>
);
```

Now, we need to replace the render function in the App component with the following:

```
render = () => (
    <HelloBox
        isExpanded={this.state.expanded}
        expandOrCollapse={this.expandOrCollapse}
    />
);
```

However, if you run the code now, you will end up with an error on the HelloText press event. This is due to how JavaScript handles the this keyword. In this refactor, we pass the expandOrCollapse function to another object, and there, this refers to a completely different object. Therefore, it cannot access state.

There are a few solutions to this problem, and one is by using the arrow function. I will stick to the best approach performance-wise. It comes down to adding the following line to your constructor:

```
this.expandOrCollapse = this.expandOrCollapse.bind(this);
```

There we go; the application is fully functional, just as before. We have refactored one component into two—one presentational and one responsible for logic. Sweet.

 Imagine that we had only shallow unit tests of two components. Would we identify the problem with the this keyword? Perhaps not. This simple gotcha may catch you in big projects, where you will be too busy to rethink every single component. Watch out and remember **integration tests**.

Decoupling styles

In the preceding examples, you may have noticed that styles are tightly coupled to presentational components. Why tightly? Because we explicitly include them by using style={styles.container}, but the styles object is not configurable. We cannot replace any style part with props, and that tightly couples us to the existing implementation. In some cases, this is a desired behavior, but in others, it is not.

 If you are interested in how styles work, we will deep dive into patterns involving them in Chapter 3, *Styling Patterns*. You will also learn about the flexbox pattern from CSS and many other conventions.

You will bump into this problem if you have tried to split code into separate files. How can we fix this issue?

Let the styles be the optional prop. If styles are not provided, then we can fall back to the default values:

```
// src/ Chapter_1/ Example_10_Decoupling_styles/ App.js
export const HelloBox = ({
    isExpanded,
    expandOrCollapse,
    containerStyles,
    expandedTextStyles
}) => (
    <View style={containerStyles || styles.container}>
        <HelloText onPress={() => expandOrCollapse()}>...</HelloText>
        <HelloText onPress={() => expandOrCollapse()}>...</HelloText>
        {
            isExpanded &&
            <HelloText style={expandedTextStyles || styles.text}>
                ...
            </HelloText>
        }
    </View>
);
```

Notice the use of the || operator. In the preceding example (expandedTextStyles || styles.text), it first checks if expandedTextStyles is defined and if so returns that value. If expandedTextStyles is undefined, then it return styles.text, which is a default style object that was hard-coded by us.

Now, if we wish, in some places, we can override our styles by passing respective props:

```
render = () => (
    <HelloBox
        isExpanded={this.state.expanded}
        expandOrCollapse={this.expandOrCollapse}
        expandedTextStyles={{ color: 'red' }}
    />
);
```

This is how we split markup, styles, and logic. Remember to use presentational components as often as possible to make your features truly reusable across many screens/views.

> If you come from a backend background, you may quickly jump into assumptions that it is just like the **MVC pattern**: **Model**, **View**, and **Controller**. It is not necessarily 1:1 relation, but in general, you may simplify it to the following:
>
> - **View**: This is a presentational component.
> - **Model**: This is a data representation, which in our case is the state that is built either in a stateful component or using so-called store and reducers (check Chapter 5, *Store Patterns*, to learn more details about what Redux is and how to use it).
> - **Controller**: This is a container component that is responsible for application logic, including event handlers and services. It should be lean and import logic from the respective files.

Container component

The container component pattern was introduced a long time ago and was popularized within the React community by Dan Abramov. So far, we have created one container component when we refactored the contents of the App component to become a *presentational component*. It turns out that the App component became a container component—it contains the HelloBox component and implements the necessary logic for it. What did we gain from this approach? We gained the following:

- We can implement expanding and collapsing in a different way and reuse the markup of the HelloBox component
- HelloBox does not contain logic

- The container component encapsulates logic and hides it from the other components

 I highly recommend reading Dan Abramov's medium post on this. Check out `https://medium.com/@dan_abramov/smart-and-dumb-components-7ca2f9a7c7d0` for more information. Container components are very useful tools when it comes to dependency injection patterns. Have a look at `Chapter 10`, *Managing Dependencies*, to learn more.

HOC

The **HOC** is a pattern that exists to enhance components with additional props or functionality, for instance, if you want to make the component expandable. Instead of just creating a stateful container as we did previously, we could use the HOC pattern. Let's refactor our stateful container component to a HOC and name it `makeExpandable`:

```
// src/ Chapter_1/ Example_12_Higher_order_component_makeExpandable/ App.js

const makeExpandable = (ComponentToEnrich) => (
    class HelloBoxContainer extends React.Component {
        constructor() {
            super();
            this.state = {
                // default state on first render
                expanded: false
            };
            this.expandOrCollapse = this.expandOrCollapse.bind(this);
        }

        expandOrCollapse() {
            // toggle expanded: true becomes false, false becomes true
            this.setState({expanded: !this.state.expanded});
        }

        render = () => (
            <ComponentToEnrich
                isExpanded={this.state.expanded}
                expandOrCollapse={this.expandOrCollapse}
            />
        );
    }
);
```

The `makeExpandable` component accepts `ComponentToEnrich`. So, we can create a root component (`App`) like this:

```
export default makeExpandable(HelloBox);
```

Cool, isn't it? Now, let's create some other component and enrich it with our HOC. This will be a small button that displays the text hide or show. If the user presses the button, it should show or hide a small colored box. For this task, you can use the following styles:

```
box: {
    width: 100,
    height: 100,
    backgroundColor: 'powderblue',
}
```

Place them within `StyleSheet.create({ ... })`. My solution is pretty straightforward:

```
// src/ Chapter_1/
// Example_13_Higher_order_component_show_hide_button/ App.js

export const SomeSection = ({
    isExpanded,
    expandOrCollapse,
    containerStyles,
    boxStyle
}) => (
    <View style={containerStyles || styles.container}>
        <Button
            onPress={expandOrCollapse}
            title={isExpanded ? "Hide" : "Show"}
            color="#841584"
        />
        {isExpanded && <View style={boxStyle || styles.box} />}
    </View>
);

export default makeExpandable(SomeSection);
```

In the preceding example, the `SomeSection` component is wrapped by the `makeExpandable` HOC, and receives the `isExpanded` and `expandOrCollapse` props.

Great! We have just made a reusable HOC, and it is working flawlessly.

Now, I will show you a rather unknown but sometimes useful technique to push your HOC to be even more flexible. Imagine that you are about to enhance a component that is strict about props naming, as in the following example:

```
export const SomeSection = ({
    showHideBox,
    isVisible,
    containerStyles,
    boxStyle
}) => {...};
```

Unfortunately, our HOC, `makeExpandable`, is passing the wrong prop names. Let's fix that:

```
// src/ Chapter_1/ Example_14_Flexible_prop_names_in_HOC/ App.js
render = () => {
  const props = {
    [propNames && propNames.isExpanded || 'isExpanded']:
this.state.expanded,
    [propNames && propNames.expandOrCollapse || 'expandOrCollapse']:
this.expandOrCollapse
  };
  return <ComponentToEnrich {...props} />
};
```

This is a tricky example. It provides a capability to rename props that are passed down by HOC. To rename it, we need to pass a configuration object called `propNames` to HOC. If such an object is passed, and it contains a certain key, then we override the name. If the key is not present, then we fall back to the default prop name, for instance, `isExpanded`.

 Notice the use of `[]` inside of the object. It allows you to dynamically name keys in the object. In this example, the key was dynamically chosen based on the presence of `propNames`.

To make everything work, we also need to accept the optional argument `propNames` in the `makeExpandable` HOC:

```
const makeExpandable = (ComponentToEnrich, propNames) => (
    ...
)
```

Cool! Now our HOC is more flexible when it comes to prop names! We can use it with the aforementioned strict `SomeSection` component:

```
export default makeExpandable(SomeSection, {
    isExpanded: 'isVisible',
    expandOrCollapse: 'showHideBox'
});
```

Beware of the performance implications when creating variables inside the `render` function. It will slow your application down. Sometimes, patterns can sacrifice performance a little and sometimes they cannot. Use them wisely. You could also the inline `propNames` variable as two props.

Make sure to check the next section for a cleaner and decoupled approach.

HOC composition

The primary reason to create HOCs it to have the ability to compose the features they provide.

Look at the problem from the previous section again. What if we could delegate work to another HOC? For instance, having a mapper HOC called `mapPropNames`, you can compose it with our previous HOC like this:

```
makeExpandable(mapPropNames(SomeSection));
```

Here is the implementation of `mapPropNames`:

```
// src/ Chapter_1/ Example_15_HOC_Composition/ App.js

const mapPropNames = (Component) => (props) => (
    <Component
        {...props}
        isVisible={props.isExpanded}
        showHideBox={props.expandOrCollapse}
    />
);
```

Nice and quick, isn't it? This is a common pattern and is also used when working with backend data sent as JSON. It may adapt the data format to our representation on the frontend layer. As you see, we can employ this great idea when working with HOCs as well!

If you come from an object-oriented background, please notice that the HOC pattern is very similar to the decorator pattern. The decorator, however, also relies on inheritance and needs to implement the interface that it decorates.

Please check https://en.wikipedia.org/wiki/Decorator_pattern for examples.

You can also compose decorators. It works in a similar way.

Examples of useful HOCs

Do you need a quick logger that will show you how your app behaves? Or maybe you are preparing a live presentation and you want to show some dynamic information on a screen? Here we go:

```
// src/ Chapter_1/ Example_16_Useful_HOCs/ App.js

const logPropChanges = Component => props => {
    console.log('[Actual props]:', props);
    return <Component {...props} />;
};
// Use: makeExpandable(logPropChanges(mapPropNames(SomeSection)));
```

Okay, good. Now, let's suppose that you are waiting on some data to load. Here comes the spinner:

```
// src/ Chapter_1/ Example_16_Useful_HOCs/ App.js

import {ActivityIndicator} from 'react-native';
const withSpinner = Component => props => (
    props.shouldSpin
        ? <View style={styles.container}>
            <Text>Your fav spinner f.in. on data load.</Text>
            <ActivityIndicator size="large" color="#0000ff" />
        </View>
        : <Component {...props} />
);
// Needs a HOC that provides prop shouldSpin (true/false)
```

You might want to ask a user to five star your app. You need a modal to do this:

```
const withModalOpener = Component => props => (
    // Replace with your favourite Modal box implementation
    <Component {...props} openModal={() => console.log('opening...')} />
);
```

Sometimes, modals should be intelligent enough to maintain their visibility, too:

```
// src/ Chapter_1/ Example_16_Useful_HOCs/ App.js

const withModalOpener = OriginalComponent => (
    class ModalExample extends React.Component {
        // Check this shorter way to init state
        state = {
            modalVisible: true,
        };

        setModalVisible(visible) {
            this.setState({modalVisible: visible});
        }

        render() {
            return (
                // Replace with your favourite Modal box implementation
                <View style={styles.container}>
                    <OriginalComponent
                        {...this.props}
                        openModal={() => this.setModalVisible(true)}
                        closeModal={() =>
                     this.setModalVisible(false)}
                    />
                    <Modal
                        animationType="slide"
                        visible={this.state.modalVisible}
                        onRequestClose={() => {
                            alert('Modal has been closed.');
                        }}>
                        <View style={styles.container}>
                            <Text>Example modal!</Text>

                            <TouchableHighlight
                                onPress={() => {
                                    this.setModalVisible(false);
                                }}>
                                <Text style={{fontSize: 30}}>
                                    Hide Modal
                                </Text>
```

```
                    </TouchableHighlight>
                </View>
            </Modal>
        </View>
    );
  }
}
);
```

In this example, we enriched the component with `Modal`. `Modal` can be opened or closed using the props that are named `openModal` and `closeModal`. The information regarding whether the modal is opened or closed is stored within a private state of the HOC and, in this example, is not exposed to the original component. Nice separation, right? This HOC is also reusable.

Time for your homework: how do we make `Modal` open along with the box show? You cannot change `SomeComponent`.

Summary

In this chapter, you have learned how to create basic components with React in the React Native environment. Now, you should be fairly comfortable with stateless and stateful components. In addition, you learned about presentational and container components. You know that these patterns serve to decouple markup and logic. You have also learned how to enhance component features by using HOCs. Hopefully, you have also played with the ready-to-run examples that I collected for you in the Git repository.

In `Chapter 2`, *View Patterns*, we will focus more on the markup. You will also learn about a handful of tags that you can use.

2
View Patterns

One very demanding skill is writing good view code the first time around. It comes with experience and becomes almost automatic at some point. Hence, it is vital to do it right from the beginning. In this chapter, we will explore best practices and go through the React JSX patterns that you already used in the previous chapter. We will also focus on the broader spectrum of built-in components, which include input and forms. At the very end, I will show you a nice tool called a linter that is essential for any new frontend project.

In this chapter, you will learn how to do the following:

- Write concise JSX
- Use common React Native built-in components
- Create simple forms using `TextInput`
- Distinguish between controlled and uncontrolled input
- Create error boundaries
- Eliminate Mixins from your code base
- Set up a linter to enforce your code style guide

Technical requirements

In this chapter, you will learn about various patterns, along with their code snippets. However, to run them, you will need the Create React Native App package. I have separated every example into a standalone application that you can launch on your phone or simulator.

To follow along with the examples in this chapter, you will need the following:

- An Android/iOS phone or simulator
- Git, to pull the examples: `https://github.com/Ajdija/hands-on-design-patterns-with-react-native`

Follow the installation and running instructions from the GitHub page to get started.

Introduction to JSX

We have been using JSX so far, but what does it mean? JSX stands for JavaScript extension. How can it be an extension?

As you probably know, ECMAScript is also an extension to JavaScript (kind of). ECMAScript transpiles to JavaScript. What does this mean? It means that it just transforms ECMAScript code into valid JavaScript code. JavaScript misses out on many features that we like from ECMAScript, such as arrow functions, classes, and destructuring operators.

JSX works the same way. JSX is being transpiled to JavaScript, and its main feature is creating React elements based on the markup you write.
Could we use only JavaScript? Yes. Is it worth it? Most likely not.

Let's check this out in action. This is JSX *and* ECMAScript:

```
export default () => <Text style={{marginTop: 30}}>Example Text!</Text>
```

Now, compare this to pure JavaScript:

```
export default function() {
    return React.createElement(
        Text,
        {style: {marginTop: 30}},
        'Example Text!'
    );
}
```

There's no doubt that the first code snippet is easier to read and understand.

 Babel transpiles JSX to JavaScript. Check out this interactive tool so that you can play around and see what the output is in more complex examples: `https://goo.gl/RjMXKC`.

JSX standard tricks

Before we proceed further, I want to show you the best practices when it comes to writing your JSX markup. This will make your journey through my further examples much easier.

Let's start with the simple rules:

- If there are no children within your component, use a self-closing tag:

```
// good
<Button onPress={handlePress} />

// bad
<Button onPress={handlePress}></Button>
```

- If you need to display a component based on some condition, then use the && operator:

```
// bad
function HelloComponent(props) {
    if (isSomeCondition) {
return <p>Hello!</p>;
    }
return null;
}

// bad
const HelloComponent = () => {
  return isSomeCondition ? <p>Hello!</p> : null
};

// ok (probably it will require some logic before return)
const HelloComponent = () => { return isSomeCondition &&
<p>Hello!</p> };

// almost good (isSomeCondition can be passed using props)
const HelloComponent = () => isSomeCondition && <p>Hello!</p>;

// best: use above solution but within encapsulating component
// this way HelloComponent is not tightly tied to isSomeCondition

const HelloComponent = () => <p>Hello!</p>;
const SomeComponent = () => (
    // <== here some component JSX ...
    isSomeCondition && <HelloComponent />
    // <== the rest of encapsulating component markup here
);
```

The preceding practices only apply if the other option is `null`. If the false case is also a component, you can use the *b ? x : y* operator or even a simple `if-else` approach, however, it should comply with your project's best practices.

- If you use the *b ? x : y* operator, then you may find that curly braces (`{ }`) come in handy:

```
const SomeComponent = (props) => (
<View>
        <Text>{props.isLoggedIn ? 'Log In' : 'Log Out'}</Text>
    </View>
);
```

- You can also use curly braces (`{ }`) to destructure props objects:

```
const SomeComponent = ({ isLoggedIn, ...otherProps }) => (
<View>
        <Text>{isLoggedIn ? 'Log In' : 'Log Out'}</Text>
    </View>
);
```

- If you want to pass `isLoggedIn` as `true`, you can do so by just writing the prop name:

```
// recommended
const OtherComponent = () => (
    <SomeComponent isLoggedIn />
);

// not recommended
const OtherComponent = () => (
    <SomeComponent isLoggedIn={true} />
);
```

- In some cases, you may want to pass on all of the other props. You can use the spread operator in such a case:

```
const SomeButton = ({ type , ...other }) => {
const className = type === "blue" ? "BlueButton" : "GrayButton";
    return <button className={className} {...other} />;
};
```

A beginner's guide to naming

Naming may sound trivial, but there are some standard practices in React that you should comply with. These practices may vary from project to project, but keep in mind that you should respect at least the ones that are mentioned here. In other cases, check your project's style guide and possibly your linter configuration.

 One of the great React style guides comes from Airbnb and can be checked out at `https://github.com/airbnb/javascript/tree/master/react#naming`.

A component name should start with an uppercase letter unless it's a HOC. Use the component name as the filename. The filename should be in UpperCamelCase (for more information on CamelCase, see `https://en.wikipedia.org/wiki/Camel_case`):

```
// bad
someSection.js
// good
SomeSection.js or SomeSection.jsx
// Current Airbnb style guide recommends .jsx extension though.
```

The following are rules on importing your component:

```
// bad
import App from './App/App';

// bad
import App from './App/index';

// good
import App from './App';
```

If it's HOC, start its name with a lowercase letter in lower CamelCase, for instance, `makeExpandable`.

Airbnb also suggests that you take care of the name of the inner component. We need to specify a `displayName` prop to do, as in the following:

```
// Excerpt from
// https://github.com/airbnb/javascript/tree/master/react#naming
// bad
export default function withFoo(WrappedComponent) {
  return function WithFoo(props) {
    return <WrappedComponent {...props} foo />;
  }
```

```
  }

// good
export default function withFoo(WrappedComponent) {
  function WithFoo(props) {
    return <WrappedComponent {...props} foo />;
  }

  const wrappedComponentName = WrappedComponent.displayName
    || WrappedComponent.name
    || 'Component';

  WithFoo.displayName = `withFoo(${wrappedComponentName})`;
  return WithFoo;
}
```

This is a valid point as in some tools you may benefit from seeing the proper component names. Following this pattern is optional and up to the team to decide upon.

 One can create a HOC that takes care of the displayName prop. Such a HOC can be reused on top of the HOCs we created in Chapter 1, *React Component Patterns*.

When defining new props, please avoid the common props that used to mean something else. An example may be the style prop we used to pass styles to our components. Please check out the following links to check what props you should avoid using:

- Props corresponding to your application layout:
  - https://facebook.github.io/react-native/docs/layout-props.html
- Props reserved for component styling, as it may create confusion:
  - https://facebook.github.io/react-native/docs/image-style-props.html
  - https://facebook.github.io/react-native/docs/text-style-props.html
  - https://facebook.github.io/react-native/docs/view-style-props.html

Don't get too scared. It will feel more natural sooner or later.

Type checking with PropTypes

React comes with support for basic type checking. It does not require you to upgrade to TypeScript or another, more advanced solution. To achieve type checking straight away, you can use the `prop-types` library.

Let's provide type definitions for our `HelloBox` component from `Chapter 1/Example 12`:

```
import PropTypes from 'prop-types';

// ...

HelloBox.propTypes = {
  isExpanded: PropTypes.bool.isRequired,
  expandOrCollapse: PropTypes.func.isRequired,
  containerStyles: PropTypes.object,
  expandedTextStyles: PropTypes.object
};
```

This way, we force `isExpanded` to be of the Boolean type (`true` or `false`), and `expandOrCollapse` to be a function. We also let React know about two optional style props (`containerStyles` and `expandedTextStyles`). If styles are not provided, we simply return the default styles.

There is also a neat feature to avoid explicit `if` in the markup—default props. Check it out:

```
HelloBox.defaultProps = {
    containerStyles: styles.container,
    expandedTextStyles: styles.text
};
```

Cool! Now, if `containerStyles` or `expandedTextStyles` are be null, then they will get a respective default value. However, if you run your application now, you will notice a little warning:

```
Warning: Failed prop type: Invalid prop `containerStyles` of type `number`
supplied to `HelloBox`, expected `object`.
```

You may be freaking out right now, but this is correct. This is a nice optimization that has been made by the React Native team that you may not be aware of. It caches the stylesheet and simply sends the cached ID. The following line is returning the number and ID of a stylesheet that represents the `styles` object that was passed:

```
styles.container
```

Hence, we need to adapt our type definitions:

```
HelloBox.propTypes = {
    isExpanded: PropTypes.bool.isRequired,
    expandOrCollapse: PropTypes.func.isRequired,
    containerStyles: PropTypes.oneOfType([
        PropTypes.object,
        PropTypes.number
    ]),
    expandedTextStyles: PropTypes.oneOfType([
        PropTypes.object,
        PropTypes.number
    ])
};
```

Now, you can remove explicit `if` statements in the component markup. It should look more or less like this:

```
export const HelloBox = ({
    isExpanded,
    expandOrCollapse,
    containerStyles,
    expandedTextStyles
}) => (
    <View style={containerStyles}>
        <HelloText onPress={() => expandOrCollapse()}>...</HelloText>
        <HelloText onPress={() => expandOrCollapse()}>...</HelloText>
        {
            isExpanded &&
            <HelloText style={expandedTextStyles}>
                ...
            </HelloText>
        }
    </View>
);
```

Good job! We have defined default props and type checks for our component. Please check the full working `Example 2` in the `src/chapter 2` directory for more details.

Please note that, from now on, all code examples will be split into a few modular source files. All files will be placed under the ./src directory of the respective example.

For instance, Example 2 is organized in the following way:

- src
  - HelloBox.js
  - HelloText.js
  - makeExpandable.js
- App.js

This structure will evolve as the application grows. In Chapter 10, *Managing Dependencies*, you will learn how to organize files in big projects with over one million lines of code.

Built-in components you need to know about

React Native is growing fast and changing often. I have selected a curated list of components that are likely to stay within the API for a long time. We will spend some time learning them so that we will be able to proceed faster later on in this book. Any further examples will rely on these components and will assume that you know what these components are for.

The ScrollView component

So far, we know about three components: View, Text, and StyleSheet. Now, imagine a case where we have a lot of rows to show in the application—something such as table of information pops into my mind. Obviously, it will be a long table, but the screen is small, so we will make it scrollable—up and down, like in a browser. This may seem trivial as a concept, but this isn't very easy to implement, which is why React Native provides the ScrollView component.

Let's see this problem in action. Check out Example 3_ No ScrollView problem from the Chapter 2 folder to get started.

Here, we have a typical `TaskList` component, which converts every task into a `Task` component. `Task` displays its name and description as `Text`. It's a very simple mechanism, but once a number of tasks is huge, such as 20 or more tasks, it fills the entire screen, and suddenly you realize that you cannot scroll like in a browser window:

```
// Chapter 2 / Example 3 / src / TaskList.js
export const TaskList = ({tasks, containerStyles}) => (
    <View style={containerStyles}>
        {tasks.map(task => // problems if task list is huge
            <ExpandableTask
                key={task.name + task.description}
                name={task.name}
                description={task.description}
            />
        )}
    </View>
);
```

To fix this issue and make the content scrollable, replace `View` with `ScrollView`. You also need to rename the `style` prop to `contentContainerStyle`. Please see the full example, as follows:

```
// Chapter 2 / Example 4 / src / TaskList.js
import React from 'react';
import Task from './Task';
import PropTypes from 'prop-types';
import {StyleSheet, Text, ScrollView, View} from 'react-native';
import makeExpandable from './makeExpandable';

const ExpandableTask = makeExpandable(Task);

export const TaskList = ({tasks, containerStyles}) => (
    <ScrollView contentContainerStyle={containerStyles}>
        {tasks.map(task =>
            <ExpandableTask
                key={task.name + task.description}
                name={task.name}
                description={task.description}
            />
        )}
    </ScrollView>
);

const styles = StyleSheet.create({
    container: {
        backgroundColor: '#fff'
    }
```

```
});

TaskList.propTypes = {
    tasks: PropTypes.arrayOf(PropTypes.shape({
        name: PropTypes.string.isRequired,
        description: PropTypes.string.isRequired
    })),
    containerStyles: PropTypes.oneOfType([
        PropTypes.object,
        PropTypes.number
    ])
};

TaskList.defaultProps = {
    tasks: [],
    containerStyles: styles.container
};

export default TaskList;
```

I have also included `PropTypes` definitions so that you can practice what we have learned in the previous section.

 Notice the use of the `key` prop (key={task.name + task.description}) on the `Task` component. This is required when you render collections so that React can distinguish elements on prop changes and, if possible, avoid unnecessary repainting of the component.

The Image component

The next component that you will often use is the `Image` component. Let's extend our task list with the React logo. After each task, we will show a `.png` image of the React logo:

```
// Chapter 2_View patterns/ Example 5/src /Task.js
// ...
<Image
    // styles just to make it smaller in the example
    style={{width: 100, height: 100}}
    source={require("./react.png")}
/>
// ...
```

Please note that not every image type is supported right now. For instance, SVG images will need a separate library to work.

You can check out the props that the `Image` component consumes in the official documentation here: `https://facebook.github.io/react-native/docs/image`. You will find useful props such as `loadingIndicatorSource` here—this is an image that is shown while a big source image is loading.

The TextInput component

We will use this component often in the next section. The general idea is to be able to pass data from a smartphone keyboard. `TextInput` is used in login and registration forms and many other places where the user needs to send text data to an application.

Let's extend the `HelloWorld` example from Chapter 1, *React Component Patterns*, to accept a name:

```
// Chapter 2 / Example 6 / src / TextInputExample.js
export default class TextInputExample extends React.Component {
    state = {
        name: null
    };

    render = () => (
        <View style={styles.container}>
            {this.state.name && (
                <Text style={styles.text}>
                    Hello {this.state.name}
                </Text>
            )}
            <Text>Hands-On Design Patterns with React Native</Text>
            <Text>Chapter 2: View Patterns</Text>
            <Text style={styles.text}>
                Enter your name below and see what happens.
            </Text>
            <TextInput
                style={styles.input}
                onChangeText={name => this.setState({name})}
            />
        </View>
    );
}
// ... styles skipped for clarity in a book, check source files.
```

If a user enters text in the `TextInput` component, then we display the entered text in a short greeting. Conditional rendering uses `state` to check whether the name has been defined or not. As the user types, the `onChangeText` event handler is invoked, and the function we passed updates the state with the new name.

 Sometimes, native keyboards may overlap with your `View` component and hide important information. Please get familiar with the `KeyboardAvoidingView` component if this is the case in your app. Check out `https://facebook.github.io/react-native/docs/keyboardavoidingview.html` for more information.

The Button component

`Button` is such a common component that you will find yourself using it in any kind of app. Let's build a small `like` counter with up and down buttons:

```
// Chapter 2 / Example 7 / src / LikeCounter.js
class LikeCounter extends React.Component {
    state = {
        likeCount: 0
    }
    // like/unlike function to increase/decrease like count in state
    like = () => this.setState({likeCount: this.state.likeCount + 1})
    unlike = () => this.setState({likeCount: this.state.likeCount - 1})

    render = () => (
        <View style={styles.container}>
            <Button
                onPress={this.unlike}
                title="Unlike"
            />
            <Text style={styles.text}>{this.state.likeCount}</Text>
            <Button
                onPress={this.like}
                title="Like"
            />
        </View>
    );
}
// Styles omitted for clarity
```

Further modifications to this concept can implement upvotes/downvotes for comments or a star system for reviews.

 The Button component is very limited, and those who are used to web development may be surprised. For instance, you cannot set the text in a web-way, for example, <Button>Like</Button>, nor can you pass the style prop. If you need to style your button, please use TouchableXXXX. Check out the next section for an example on TouchableOpacity.

Touchable opacity

When a button needs a custom look, it quickly seems like you need a better alternative. This is where TouchableOpacity comes into play. It serves every purpose when inner content needs to become touchable. Hence, we will make our own button and style it as we like:

```
class LikeCounter extends React.Component {
    state = {
        likeCount: 0
    }
    like = () => this.setState({likeCount: this.state.likeCount + 1})
    unlike = () => this.setState({likeCount: this.state.likeCount - 1})

    render = () => (
        <View style={styles.container}>
            <TouchableOpacity
                style={styles.button}
                onPress={this.unlike}
            >
                <Text>Unlike</Text>
            </TouchableOpacity>
            <Text style={styles.text}>{this.state.likeCount}</Text>
            <TouchableOpacity
                style={styles.button}
                onPress={this.like}
            >
                <Text>Like</Text>
            </TouchableOpacity>
        </View>
    );
}
```

Some example styles follow. We will dig further into styles in Chapter 3, *Styling Patterns*:

```
const styles = StyleSheet.create({
    container: {
```

```
            flexDirection: 'row',
            paddingTop: 20,
            paddingLeft: 20
    },
    button: {
        alignItems: 'center', // horizontally centered
        justifyContent: 'center', // vertically centered
        backgroundColor: '#DDDDDD',
        padding: 20
    },
    text: {
        fontSize: 45
    }
});
```

The button's contents are centered vertically and horizontally. We have a custom gray background color and padding inside of the button. Padding is the space from the children to the border of the component.

Now that we know about these simple components, we are ready to proceed further and explore how forms are built and how to handle more complicated use cases.

Building forms

In this section, we will explore how we can handle text input from users. Traditional means of collecting input from so-called forms is divided into two major ways: controlled and uncontrolled. In a native environment, this means either handling any keypress on the React Native side (*controlled input*), or letting it be handled on the native system level and collecting data in React on demand (*uncontrolled input*).

 If you come from a web development background, please note that, at the time of writing this book, there is no form component, and I don't see it coming. There are also limitations to refs and what you can do with them. For instance, you cannot ask a ref to a TextInput for its current value. Please follow the following two subsections for more details. You can also use custom libraries, but I will not discuss such solutions here as these tend to change often.

Controlled inputs

Controlled inputs are those which handle all user input on the JavaScript side, most likely in the React state or some other state alternative (see Chapter 5, *Store Patterns*, for more information). This means that, as the user types, the keystrokes are remembered on both the native system level and the JavaScript level. This, of course, may be ineffective and should not be used in complicated UIs, which appear to be rare in the mobile world.

Do you remember the *hello world with your name* example from earlier in this chapter? This is a perfect example of controlled input. Let's see it again:

```
// Chapter 2_ View patterns/Example 6/src/TextInputExample.js

export default class TextInputExample extends React.Component {
    state = {
        name: null
    };

    render = () => (
        <View style={styles.container}>
            {this.state.name && (
                <Text style={styles.text}>
                    Hello {this.state.name}
                </Text>
            )}
            ...
            <TextInput
                style={styles.input}
                onChangeText={name => this.setState({name})}
            />
        </View>
    );
}
```

We listen on every change in the text (onChangeText) and then immediately update the component state (this.setState({name})). State becomes a single source of truth. We do not need to ask for a native component value. We only care about what is in the state. Hence, we use state to display the new Hello message, along with the typed text.

Let's see how it works in a more complex example. Our task is to create a login form with a login `TextInput`, password `TextInput`, and a `Button` component with the displayed text **Login**. Upon a user pressing the button, it should log information to our debug console. In a real application, you would pass the login details to the server to verify and then log the user in. You will learn how to do this in Chapter 5, *Store Patterns,* when we talk about side effects:

```
// Chapter 2 / Example 9 / src / LoginForm.js

export default class LoginForm extends React.Component {
    // Initial state for our components
    state = {
        login: this.props.initLogin || '', // remembered login or ''
        password: ''
    };
    // Submit handler when the Login button is pressed
    submit = () => {
        console.log(this.state.login);
        console.log(this.state.password);
    };

    render() {
        return (
            <View style={styles.container}>
                <View>
                    <TextInput
                        style={styles.input}
                        placeholder={'Login'}
                        onChangeText={login => this.setState({login})}
                    />
                </View>
                <View>
                    <TextInput
                        style={styles.input}
                        placeholder={'Password'}
                        onChangeText={
                            password => this.setState({password})
                        }
                        secureTextEntry={true} // hide password
                    />
                </View>
                <View>
                    <Button
                        onPress={this.submit}
                        title="Login"
                    />
                </View>
```

```
            </View>
        );
    }
}
```

Please note three important things here:

- It provides the ability to pass remembered login text. The complete feature would require remembering the login on the physical device memory, and so I omitted this for clarity.
- The `secureTextEntry` prop of `TextInput` that hides the password behind dots.
- The `onPress` handler on the button component so that it can do something with the collected data. In this simple example, we just log to the debug console.

Uncontrolled input

Uncontrolled input in React Native is not really what it is in web development. In fact, `TextInput` cannot be uncontrolled entirely. You need to listen to a value change in some way:

- `onChangeText` fires every time the text input changes
- `onSubmitEditing` fires when the text input's submit button is pressed

Additionally, `TextInput` by itself is a controlled component. Check further for an explanation. A long time ago, it used to have a prop called `controlled` that allowed you to specify a Boolean value, but this has changed. The documentation at that time specified the following:

> *"If you really want this to behave as a controlled component, you can set this to true, but you will probably see flickering, dropped keystrokes, and/or laggy typing, depending on how you process onChange events."*
> —https://facebook.github.io/react-native/docs/0.7/textinput.html.

I realize that the React Native team did put a lot of effort into addressing these issues and they fixed `TextInput`. However, `TextInput` became a controlled input to some extent. For instance, selection on `TextInput` is managed by React Native within the `componentDidUpdate` function.

> *"Selection is also a controlled prop. If the native value doesn't match JS, update to the JS value."*

— React Native source code for TextInput: `https://github.com/react-native/blob/c595509048cc5f6cab360cd2ccbe7c86405baf92/Libraries/Components/TextInput/TextInput.js`.

Unless you specify the `onChangeText` or `value` props, then your component does not appear to get any more overhead.

The fact is that you can still use refs. Check out the following example to learn how to use React's latest API:

```
// Chapter 2 / Example 10 / App.js

export default class App extends React.Component {
    constructor(props) {
        super(props);

        this.inputRef = React.createRef();
    }

    render = () => (
        <TextInput style={{height:50}} ref={ref => this.inputRef = ref} />
    );

    componentDidMount() {
        this.inputRef.focus();
    }
}
```

However, there are some limitations. You cannot ask ref for the input value. Sadly, I find this unlikely to change. If you look at this from the other side, it feels more natural. You probably only need controlled components. The benefit from uncontrolled ones is performance that, as of now, does not differ much. Hence, I doubt that you need uncontrolled components in React Native. I couldn't even come up with a use case where you would need a lot of uncontrolled components because of performance issues.

The closest I could get to leaving a component on its own was by using `onSubmitEditing` or `onEndEditing`. Such callbacks can be used like the `onChangeText` prop. They do not fire until the user presses the **Submit/Return** button on the native keyboard. Unfortunately, you can probably imagine the case when the user, instead of pressing the expected button, presses the login button instead. In such a case, the state would not be updated with the latest data, because the native keyboard remains opened. Such nuances may lead to incorrect data submission and critical bugs. Be careful.

If you are developing websites using React, don't get discouraged by this section. refs are powerful for brown field websites and are useful for those who cannot afford to rewrite existing pieces into React. If this is your case, please also check out the portals API from React v16 `https://reactjs. org/docs/portals.html`.

Introduction to error boundaries

This is quite an overlooked feature that came with React version 16. As you should already know, JavaScript can throw errors. Such errors should not break your app, especially if it is from the financial sector. The regular imperative solution from JavaScript is a `try-catch` block:

```
try {
    // helloWorld function can potentially throw error
    helloWorld();
} catch (error) {
    // If helloWorld throws error
    // we catch it and handle gracefully
    // ...
}
```

This approach is hard to use with JSX. Hence, the React team developed an alternative solution for React views. It's called `Error Boundaries`. Any class component can become an `ErrorBoundary` component, given that it implements the `componentDidCatch` function:

```
class AppErrorBoundary extends React.Component {
    state = { hasError: false };

    componentDidCatch() {
        this.setState({ hasError: true });
    }

    render = () => (
        this.state.hasError
            ? <Text>Something went wrong.</Text>
            : this.props.children
    )
}

export default () => (
    <AppErrorBoundary>
        <LoginForm />
```

```
    </AppErrorBoundary>
)
```

 If you follow along with these examples, you may see a red screen with an error nonetheless. This is a default behavior in development mode. You will have to dismiss the screen to see what the app looks like: the error boundary will work as expected. If you switch to release mode, the error screen will not appear.

LoginForm is now wrapped into ErrorBoundary. It catches any error that occurs while rendering LoginForm. If Error is caught, we display a short message stating that Something went wrong. We can get a real error message from the error object. However, it is not good practice to share it with the end user. Instead, send it to your analytics server:

```
// Chapter 2_View patterns/Example 11/ App.js
...
componentDidCatch(error) {
    this.setState({
        hasError: true,
        errorMsg: error
    });
}

render = () => (
    this.state.hasError
        ? (
            <View>
                <Text>Something went wrong.</Text>
                <Text>{this.state.errorMsg.toString()}</Text>
            </View>
        )
        : this.props.children
)
...
```

How error boundaries catch errors

It appears that error boundaries are meant to catch runtime errors that prevent rendering to finish successfully. Hence, they are very specific to React and are implemented using a special life cycle hook of the class component.

Error boundaries do not catch errors for the following:

- Event handlers
- Asynchronous code (for example, setTimeout or requestAnimationFrame callbacks)
- Server-side rendering
- Errors thrown in the error boundary itself (rather than its children)

- React official documentation at `https://reactjs.org/docs/error-boundaries.html`.

Let's discuss the previously mentioned error boundaries limitations further:

- **Event handlers**: This limitation is due to event handlers asynchronous nature. Callbacks are being invoked by an external function, and the event object is passed to a callback as a parameter. We do not have any control over this and when this will happen. The code is executed and never goes into the catch clause. Hint: This also impacts `try-catch` in the same way.
- **Asynchronous code**: Most asynchronous code will not work with error boundaries. The exception to this rule is asynchronous render functions, which will come with future releases of React.
- **Server-side rendering**: This usually concerns server-side rendered websites. Such websites are computed on the server and sent to the browser. Thanks to this, a user can immediately see the website's content. Most of the time, such server responses are cached and reused.
- **Errors thrown in the error boundary itself**: You cannot catch errors that occur within the same class component. Hence, error boundaries should contain as little logic as possible. I always recommend using a separate component for them.

Understanding error boundaries

Error boundaries can be placed in many different fashions, and each approach has its own benefits. Choose one that fits your use case. For ideas, skip to the next section. Here, we will demonstrate how the app behaves, depending on the placement of the error boundaries.

This first example uses two error boundaries around the `LikeCounter` component. If one of the `LikeCounter` components crashes, the other one will still be shown:

```
. . .
    <AppErrorBoundary>
        <LikeCounter />
    </AppErrorBoundary>
    <AppErrorBoundary>
        <LikeCounter />
    </AppErrorBoundary>
. . .
```

This second example uses one `ErrorBoundary` around two `LikeCounter` components. If one crashes, the other one will also be replaced by `ErrorBoundary`:

```
. . .
    <AppErrorBoundary>
        <LikeCounter />
        <LikeCounter />
    </AppErrorBoundary>
. . .
```

When to use error boundaries

`ErrorBoundary` is a great pattern for sure. It takes the `try-catch` concept into declarative JSX. The first time I saw it, I immediately came up with the idea to wrap the whole application into a boundary. This is fine, but it is not the only use case.

Consider the following use cases for error boundaries:

- **Widgets**: Given some incorrect data, your widget may run into problems. If, in the worst case scenario, it cannot handle the data, it may throw an error. You will want the rest of the app to be usable, given that this widget is not crucial for the rest of the application. Your analytics code should collect the error and save at least a stack trace so that the developers can fix it.
- **Modals**: Preserve the rest of the application from the faulty modal. These are usually meant to display some data and short messages. You do not want a modal to blow up your application. Such errors should be considered very rare, but *better safe than sorry*.

- **Boundaries on feature containers:** Let's say that your app is divided into major features that are represented by container components. For example, let's take a messaging app such as Facebook Messenger. You may add error boundaries to the sidebar, my story bar, footer, start new message button, and messages history list view. This will ensure that, if one feature breaks, the others have a chance to still work properly.

Now we know about all of the pros, let's discuss the cons ones: Mixins.

Why Mixins are anti-patterns

With a Mixin pattern, you mix in a certain behavior with your React components. You kind of inject a behavior for free, and you can reuse the same Mixin in different components. This all sounds great, but it isn't – and you will easily find articles on why. Here, I want to show you this anti-pattern by example.

Mixin example

Instead of shouting *Mixins are harmful,* let's create a component that is using them and look at what the issues are. Mixins are deprecated, so the first step is finding a way to use them. It turns out that they still live in a legacy way of creating React class components. Previously, instead of ES6 classes, there was a special function called `createReactClass`. In one of the major releases, the function was removed from the React library and is now available in a separate library called `'create-react-class'`:

```
// Chapter 2_View patterns/Example 12/App.js
...
import createReactClass from 'create-react-class';

const LoggerMixin = {
    componentDidMount: function() { // uses lifecycle method to log
        console.log('Component has been rendered successfully!');
    }
};

export default createReactClass({
    mixins: [LoggerMixin],
    render: function() {
        return (
            <View>
                <Text>Some text in a component with mixin.</Text>
            </View>
```

```
        );
    }
});
```

Here, we create `LoggerMixin`, which is taking care of logging the necessary information. In this simple example, it's just information regarding that component that has been rendered, but it could be easily extended further.

 In this example, we used `componentDidMount`, which is one of the component life cycle hooks. These can be used in ES6 classes, too. Please check out the official documentation for insights about the other methods: `https://reactjs.org/docs/react-component.html#the-component-lifecycle`.

In case you need more loggers, you can mix them into a single component by using a comma:

```
...
mixins: [LoggerMixin, LoggerMixin2],
...
```

 This is a book on patterns, so it is crucial to stop here and look at the `createReactClass` function.

Why has it been deprecated? The answer is actually pretty simple. The React Team prefers explicit APIs over implicit APIs. The `CreateReactClass` function is another implicit abstraction that hides implementation details from you. Instead of adding a new function, it is better to use the standard way: ES6 classes. ES6 classes have their own cons, but that is another topic entirely. Additionally, you may use classes in other languages that are built on top of ECMAScript, for instance, TypeScript. This is a huge advantage, especially nowadays, with TypeScript going mainstream.

To find out more on this thought process, I recommend that you watch a great talk from Sebastian Markbåge called **Minimal API Surface Area**. It was originally delivered at JSConf EU in 2014, and can be found at `https://www.youtube.com/watch?v=4anAwXYqLG8`.

Using HOCs instead

I believe that you can easily translate the preceding use case into HOC. Let's do this together, and then we will discuss why HOCs are better:

```
// Chapter 2_View patterns/ Example 13/ App.js
const withLogger = (ComponentToEnrich, logText) =>
    class WithLogger extends React.Component {
        componentDidMount = () => console.log(
            logText || 'Component has been rendered successfully!'
        );

        render = () => <ComponentToEnrich {...this.props} />;
    };

const App = () => (
    <View style={styles.container}>
        <Text>Some text in a component with mixin.</Text>
    </View>
);

export default withLogger(withLogger(App), 'Some other log msg');
```

The first thing you will immediately spot is that HOCs stack on top of each other. HOCs literally compose with each other. This is much more flexible and protects you from name clashes that may happen when using Mixins. React developers mention the `handleChange` function as a problematic example:

> *"There is no guarantee that two particular mixins can be used together. For example, if FluxListenerMixin defines handleChange() and WindowSizeMixin defines handleChange(), you can't use them together. You also can't define a method with this name on your own component.*
>
> *It's not a big deal if you control the mixin code. When you have a conflict, you can rename that method on one of the mixins. However, it's tricky because some components or other mixins may already be calling this method directly, and you need to find and fix those calls as well."*
>
> *- Official React blog post by Dan Abramov* (`https://reactjs.org/blog/2016/07/13/mixins-considered-harmful.html`).

Additionally, Mixins may lead to adding more and more state. Looking at the preceding examples, it may appear that HOCs do the same, but in fact, shouldn't. This is an issue that I struggle with in the React ecosystem. It gives you a lot of power and you may not realize that the patterns you begin to use are so-so. To me, stateful components should be rare, and so should stateful HOCs. In this book, I will teach you how to avoid using state objects in favor of a better solution that decouples state from your components as much as possible. We will learn about this further in Chapter 5, *Store Patterns*.

Linters and code style guide

In this section, we will take a look at quite a different set of patterns, namely, patterns on how to structure your code. Over the years, there have been tens of approaches to styling, and the general rule is this: the more people, the more preferred ways there are.

Hence, the **crucial point** of setting up the project is **selecting your style guide**, and your set of defined and precise rules. This will save enormous amounts of time for you as it removes any potential discussion.

In an era of advanced IDEs, it is possible to quickly reformat a whole code base in seconds. This will come in handy in case you need to allow for small future changes to the style of your code.

Adding a linter to create a React Native app

Follow these steps to configure your own linter:

1. Open a terminal and navigate to the project directory. The cd command for changing the directory will come in handy.
2. List (ls) the files in the directory and make sure that you are in the root and that you can see the package.json file.
3. Add the following packages by using the yarn add command. The newly added packages will be automatically added to package.json. --dev installs it under the development dependencies within package.json:

```
yarn add --dev eslint eslint-config-airbnb eslint-plugin-import
eslint-plugin-react eslint-plugin-jsx-a11y babel-eslint
```

ESLint is the linter that we will be using, and by running the preceding command, you will have installed it in the node_modules directory of your project.

4. Now, we are ready to define a new script for your project. Please edit `package.json` and add the following line under the `scripts` section:

```
"scripts": {
...
 "lint": "./node_modules/eslint/bin/eslint.js src"
...
}
```

The preceding command runs ESLint and passes one argument to it. This argument is the name of the directory that will contain files to lint. If you aren't going to follow along with this book, we are using the `src` directory to store source JavaScript files.

5. The next step is specifying a code style—more precisely, a linter configuration that implements your code style. In this example, we will use a well-known Airbnb style guide. However, we will also tweak it to adhere to my preferred style.

Firstly, create your linter configuration by running the following command:

```
./node_modules/eslint/bin/eslint.js --init
```

6. A special prompt will follow. Choose the following options:

```
How would you like to configure ESLint? Use a popular style guide
Which style guide do you want to follow? Airbnb
Do you use React? Yes
What format do you want your config file to be in? JSON
```

7. A configuration file will be created for you called `.eslintrc.json`. Open the file and add the following rules. In the next section, I will explain these choices. For now, proceed with the given set of rules:

```
{
  "rules": {
    "react/jsx-filename-extension": [1, { "extensions": [".js"] }],
    "comma-dangle": ["error", "never"],
    "no-use-before-define": ["error", { "variables": false }],
    "indent": ["error", 4],
    "react/jsx-indent": ["error", 4],
    "react/jsx-indent-props": ["error", 4]
  },
  "parser": "babel-eslint", // usage with babel transpiler
  "extends": "airbnb"
}
```

8. Now, you can run the linter by using the following command:

```
yarn run lint
```

The complete setup is provided in Example 14 under the Chapter 2_View patterns folder.

Airbnb React style guide rules

The Airbnb React style guide defines tens of well-thought-out rules. This is a great resource and a foundation for your next React project. I highly recommend looking into them. You can find the Airbnb React style guide at https://github.com/airbnb/javascript/tree/master/react.

However, everyone should find their own style. Mine just adapts a few things from the Airbnb:

- comma-dangle: Airbnb advises that you leave a trailing comma at the end of array multiline elements, lists, or object multiline key-value lists. This is not what I'm used to. I prefer the JSON style, which does not leave a trailing comma:

```
// My preference
const hero = {
  firstName: 'Dana',
  lastName: 'Scully'
};

const heroes = [
  'Batman',
  'Superman'
];

// Airbnb style guide
const hero = {
  firstName: 'Dana',
  lastName: 'Scully',
};

const heroes = [
  'Batman',
  'Superman',
];
```

- `react/jsx-filename-extension`: In my opinion, this rule should be changed in the style guide. It tries to convince you to use the `.jsx` extension for files using JSX. I don't agree with this. I would like to quote Dan Abramov's comment on this matter:

  > *"The distinction between .js and .jsx files was useful before Babel, but it's not that useful anymore.*
  >
  > *There are other syntax extensions (for example, Flow). What would you call a JS file that uses Flow? .flow.js? What about a JSX file that uses Flow? .flow.jsx? What about some other experimental syntax? .flow.stage-1.jsx?*
  >
  > *Most editors are configurable, so you can tell them to use a JSX-capable syntax scheme for .js files. Since JSX (or Flow) are strict supersets of JS, I don't see this as an issue."*
  >
  > *– Dan Abramov:* `https://github.com/facebook/create-react-app/` `issues/87#issuecomment-234627904`.

- `no-use-before-define`: This is a smart rule. It prevents you from using variables and functions that are defined later, besides the fact that the JavaScript hoisting mechanism lets you to do so. However, I like to put my StyleSheets in the bottom on every component file. Hence, I have relaxed this rule to allow usage of variables before their definition.

I also prefer an indentation of four spaces for clarity when I copy snippets into this book.

Fixing errors

As we have a linter set up, we can try it on one of the previous projects.

 If you want to follow along with this example, just copy `Example 9_Controlled TextInput` from `Chapter 2`, *View Patterns*, and set up a linter in that copied project. After that, follow with the following command, which executes your linter script on the source directory.

I tried it on `LoginForm.js` from `Example 9_ Controlled TextInput`. Unfortunately, it listed a few errors:

```
$ yarn run lint
yarn run v1.5.1
$ ./node_modules/eslint/bin/eslint.js src

/Users/mateuszgrzesiukiewicz/Work/reactnativebook/src/Chapter 2: View
patterns/Example 14: Linter/src/LoginForm.js
  2:8    error    A space is required after '{'           object-curly-
spacing
  2:44   error    A space is required before '}'          object-curly-
spacing
  7:27   error    'initLogin' is missing in props validation   react/prop-
types
  12:9   warning  Unexpected console statement             no-console
  13:9   warning  Unexpected console statement             no-console
  22:37  error    Curly braces are unnecessary here        react/jsx-
curly-brace-presence
  23:62  error    A space is required after '{'           object-curly-
spacing
  23:68  error    A space is required before '}'          object-curly-
spacing
  29:37  error    Curly braces are unnecessary here        react/jsx-
curly-brace-presence
  31:55  error    A space is required after '{'           object-curly-
spacing
  31:64  error    A space is required before '}'          object-curly-
spacing
  33:25  error    Value must be omitted for boolean attributes  react/jsx-
boolean-value
  49:20  error    Unexpected trailing comma                comma-dangle

✖ 13 problems (11 errors, 2 warnings)
  10 errors, 0 warnings potentially fixable with the `--fix` option.
```

13 problems! Luckily, ESLint may attempt to fix them automatically. Let's try. Execute the following:

```
$ yarn run lint -- --fix
```

Lovely —we reduced the issues to just three:

```
7:27 error 'initLogin' is missing in props validation react/prop-types
12:9 warning Unexpected console statement no-console
13:9 warning Unexpected console statement no-console
```

We can skip the last two. Those warnings are relevant, but the console is handy for this book: it provides an easy way to print information. Do not use `console.log` in production. However, `'initLogin' is missing in props validation react/prop-types` is a valid error, and we need to fix it:

```
LoginForm.propTypes = {
    initLogin: PropTypes.string
};
```

`LoginForm` now has its props validated. This will fix the linter error. To check this, rerun the linter. It looks like we have run into yet another issue! Correct:

```
error: propType "initLogin" is not required, but has no corresponding
defaultProp declaration react/require-default-props
```

This is true—we should have defined default props in case `initLogin` is not provided:

```
LoginForm.defaultProps = {
    initLogin: ''
};
```

From now on, if we do not explicitly provide `initLogin`, it will be assigned a default value, that is, an empty string. Rerun the linter. It will now show a new error:

```
error 'prop-types' should be listed in the project's dependencies. Run 'npm
i -S prop-types' to add it import/no-extraneous-dependencies
```

At least it's an easy one. It correctly advises you to maintain `prop-types` dependencies explicitly.

Add the `prop-types` dependency by running the following command in your console:

```
yarn add prop-types
```

Rerun the linter. Great! Finally, there are no errors. Good job.

Summary

In this chapter, we learned about view patterns that will be very useful later on in this book. Now we know how to write concise JSX and type check components. We can also compose common built-in components from the React Native library. When we need to, we can write the markup of a simple form and know how to handle the input. We compared controlled and uncontrolled inputs and dove deep into how `TextInput` works. If some errors occur, our error boundaries will handle the problem.

Finally, we made sure that we have a strict style guide on how to write React Native code, and we enforced these rules by using ESLint.

In the next chapter, we will work on styling the components we have learned. Thanks to this, our application will look nice and professional.

3
Styling Patterns

It's time to add some looks to our applications. In this chapter, we will explore unique styling solutions and mechanisms. React Native StyleSheet may resemble web **cascading style sheets (CSS)**; however, Native application styling is different. Similarities in the syntax quickly end and you should spend some time with this chapter to learn the basics of styling. Later on in this book, we will use an external library that provides ready-made styles. It is crucial for you to understand how to make such components yourself, especially if you plan to work professionally in React Native in teams who deliver custom designs.

In this chapter, we will cover the following topics:

- Styling components in the React Native environment
- Dealing with limited style inheritance
- Using density-independent pixels
- Positioning elements with Flexbox
- Handling long text issues
- Making animations using the Animated library
- Measuring your application's speed using the **Frames Per Second (FPS)** metric

Technical requirements

As in the previous chapters, I have separated every example into a standalone application that you can launch on your phone or simulator. To do the examples, you will need the following:

- Simulator or Android/iOS smartphone
- Git to pull the examples: `https://github.com/Ajdija/hands-on-design-patterns-with-react-native`. Follow the installation instructions from the GitHub page.

How React Native styles work

"The core premise for React is that UIs are simply a projection of data into a different form of data. The same input gives the same output. A simple pure function."

- React library README (`https://github.com/reactjs/react-basic/blob/`
`master/README.md`*).*

You will learn about pure functions later in this book. Check out the following example to understand the basics:

```
// Code example from React readme. Comments added for clarity.

// JavaScript pure function
// for a given input always returns the same output
function NameBox(name) {
    return { fontWeight: 'bold', labelContent: name };
}

// Example with input
'Sebastian Markbåge' ->
{ fontWeight: 'bold', labelContent: 'Sebastian Markbåge' };
```

Going back to more practical examples, let's see how the preceding premise is implemented in React Native.

"With React Native, you don't use a special language or syntax for defining styles. You just style your application using JavaScript. All of the core components accept a prop named `style`*. The style names and values usually match how CSS works on the web, except names are written using camel casing, e.g backgroundColor rather than background-color.*

The style prop can be a plain old JavaScript object. (...) You can also pass an array of styles - the last style in the array has precedence, so you can use this to inherit styles.

As a component grows in complexity, it is often cleaner to use StyleSheet.create to define several styles in one place."

- React Native official documentation (`https://facebook.github.io/react-native/`
`docs/style.html`*).*

To sum up, we have three ways of defining the component style:

- Using style props and passing an object with key-value pairs that represent styles.
- Using style props and passing an array of objects. Each object should contain key-value pairs that represent styles. The last style in the array has precedence. Use this mechanism to inherit styles or shadow them as you would shadow functions and variables.
- Using the StyleSheet component and its `create` function to create styles.

In the following example, you can find all three ways of defining styles:

```
// src/ Chapter_3/ Example_1_three_ways_to_define_styles/ App.js

export default () => (
    <View>
        <Text style={{ color: 'green' }}>inline object green</Text>
        <Text style={styles.green}>styles.green green</Text>
        <Text style={[styles.green, styles.bigred]}>
            [styles.green, styles.bigred] // big red
        </Text>
        <Text style={[styles.bigred, styles.green]}>
            [styles.bigred, styles.green] // big green
        </Text>
    </View>
);

const styles = StyleSheet.create({
    green: {
        color: 'green'
    },
    bigred: {
        color: 'red',
        fontSize: 35
    }
});
```

Pay attention to the use case with array of objects. You may combine previously-learned tricks to achieve conditional styles:

```
<View>
    <Text
        style={[
            styles.linkStyle,
            this.props.isActive && styles.activeLink
        ]}
    >
```

```
        Some link
    </Text>
</View>
```

Also, let's discuss why we use the `StyleSheet` component instead of inline styles:

- Code quality:
    - By moving styles away from the render function, you're making the code easier to understand.
    - Naming the styles is a good way to add meaning to the low-level components in the render function.

- Performance:
    - Making a `stylesheet` from a `style` object makes it possible to refer to it by ID instead of creating a new style object every time.
    - It also allows you to send the style only once through the bridge. All subsequent uses are going to refer an ID (not implemented yet).

    - React Native official documentation
    `https://facebook.github.io/react-native/docs/stylesheet.html.`

When it comes to the quality and reusability, StyleSheet decouples styles and component markup. You could even extract these styles away to a separate file. Also, as mentioned in the documentation, it allows you to make your markup easier to understand. Instead of a huge styling object, you can see a meaningful name, such as `styles.activeLink`.

 If you undervalue decoupling in your applications, then try to grow your code base beyond 5,000 lines. You will likely see that some tightly-coupled code will need hacks to be reusable. Bad practices will snowball, making the code base very hard to maintain. In backend systems, it usually goes hand-in-hand with monolithic structures. The amazing idea that comes to the rescue is Microservices. Learn more at `https://en.wikipedia.org/wiki/Microservices`.

Surprising styles inheritance

As we start to use styles, it is vital to understand that React Native styles do not work as a website's CSS. Especially when it comes to inheritance.

Styles of the parent component are not inherited unless it is a Text component. If it is a Text component, it will inherit from parent, only if parent is another Text component:

```
// src/ Chapter_3/ Example_2_Inheritance_of_Text_component/ App.js

export default () => (
    <View style={styles.container}>
        <Text style={styles.green}>
            some green text
            <Text style={styles.big}>
                some big green text
            </Text>
        </Text>
    </View>
);

const styles = StyleSheet.create({
    container: {
        marginTop: 40
    },
    green: {
        color: 'green'
    },
    big: {
        fontSize: 35
    }
});
```

If you run this code, you will see that the displayed text is green and that the later part is also big. Text with a big style inherited the green colour from the parent Text component. Please also note that the whole text is rendered inside of a View component that has a margin top of 40 dp that is density-independent pixels. Jump to the *Learning unitless dimensions* section to learn more.

Workaround for limited inheritance

Imagine a situation where you would like to reuse the same font across the whole application. Given the mentioned inheritance limitations, how would you do that?

The solution is a mechanism that we have learned already: component composition. Let's create a component that satisfies our requirements:

```
// src/ Chapter_3/ Example_3/ src/ AppText.js

const AppText = ({ children, ...props }) => (
    <Text style={styles.appText} {...props}>
        {children}
    </Text>
);
// ... propTypes and defaultProps omitted for clarity

const styles = StyleSheet.create({
    appText: {
        fontFamily: 'Verdana'
    }
});

export default AppText;
```

The `AppText` component just wraps the `Text` component and specifies its styles. In this simple example, it's just `fontFamily`.

> Please note that the `fontFamily` key in `style` object accepts String values and may differ between platforms (some are accepted on Android and some are accepted on iOS). For consistency, you may need to use a custom font. The setup is rather easy but takes a while and so exceeds the design patterns topic of this book. To learn more, visit `https://docs.expo.io/versions/latest/guides/using-custom-fonts`.

Think about how to edit `AppText` to support custom styles so that it will be possible to override specified keys.

Is the style object override the best solution in this case? Perhaps not; you have created this component to unify styles, not to allow overrides. But, you may say that it could be needed to create another component, such as `HeaderText` or something similar. You need a way to reuse existing styles and still enlarge the text. Luckily, you can still use `Text` inheritance here:

```
// src / Chapter 3 / Example 3 / App.js
export default () => (
    <View style={styles.container}>
        <AppText>
            some text, Verdana font
            <Text style={styles.big}>
                some big text, Verdana font
```

```
            </Text>
        </AppText>
        <Text style={styles.big}>
            some normal big text
        </Text>
    </View>
);
```

Hence, `HeaderText` would be very simple to implement. Check the following code:

```
// src / Chapter 3 / Example 3 / src / HeaderText.js
const HeaderText = ({ children, ...props }) => (
    <AppText>
        <Text style={styles.headerText} {...props}>
            {children}
        </Text>
    </AppText>
);
// ...
const styles = StyleSheet.create({
    headerText: {
        fontSize: 30
    }
});
```

Learning unitless dimensions

In this section, we will learn the dimensions in which React Native applications are measured onscreen.

> *"The simplest way to set the dimensions of a component is by adding a fixed width and height to style. All dimensions in React Native are unitless, and represent density-independent pixels."*
>
> *- React Native official documentation*
> `https://facebook.github.io/react-native/docs/height-and-width.html`.

Unlike in CSS, for style properties such as `margin`, `bottom`, `top`, `left`, `right`, `height`, and `width`, you must provide values in dp or percentages.

That's it for the documentation. But you also need to understand the following keywords when it comes to working with screens:

- **Pixels**: These are the smallest single elements of the screen that can be controlled. Each pixel usually consists of three sub-pixels: red, green, and blue. These colors are usually referred to as RGB.
- **Dimensions**: These are the width and height of the screen or window.
- **Resolution**: This is the number of pixels in each dimension that can be displayed.
- **DPI/PPI**: This is the number of dots/pixels that can be placed per one inch.
- **Points**: This is an abstract measurement for iOS.
- **Density-independent pixels**: This is an abstract measurement for Android.

If you want to check how these concepts are implemented in Java, have a look at:
`https://github.com/facebook/react-native/blob/master/ReactAndroid/src/main/java/com/facebook/react/uimanager/LayoutShadowNode.java`.

To calculate the values, we will need `width`, `height`, and `scale`. You can get this information from the `Dimensions` object:

```
// src/ Chapter 3/ Example 4/ App.js

export default () => {
    const { height, width } = Dimensions.get('window');
    return (
        <View style={{ marginTop: 40 }}>
            <Text>Width: {width}, Height: {height}</Text>
            <View
                style={{
                    width: width / 4,
                    height: height / 3,
                    backgroundColor: 'steelblue'
                }}
            />
            <View style={styles.powderblue} />
        </View>
    );
};

const styles = StyleSheet.create({
    powderBlueBox: {
        width: Dimensions.get('window').width / 2,
        height: Dimensions.get('window').height / 5,
        backgroundColor: 'powderblue'
```

```
    }
});
```

However, this code is broken. Can you see why? It does not update if you rotate the device.

We need to force a re-render if the dimensions change. We can detect a dimension change by registering our own listener using `Dimensions.addEventListener`. Then we need to force a re-render in this listener. Usually people use `state` to do so. React checks `state` for changes and re-renders if that happens:

```
// src/ Chapter_3/ Example_5_Listening_on_dimensions_change/ App.js

export default class LogDimensionChanges extends React.Component {
    state = { window: Dimensions.get('window') };
    componentWillMount() {
        // This lifecycle hook runs before component
        // is render for the first time
        Dimensions.addEventListener('change', this.handler);
    }
    componentWillUnmount() {
        // This lifecycle hook runs after unmount
        // that is when component is removed
        // It is important to remove listener to prevent memory leaks
        Dimensions.removeEventListener('change', this.handler);
    }
    handler = dims => this.setState(dims);

    render() {
        const { width, height } = this.state.window;
        return (
            ...
                <View
                    style={{
                        width: width / 4,
                        height: height / 3,
                        backgroundColor: 'steelblue'
                    }}
                />
                <View style={styles.powderBlueBox} />
            ...
        );
    }
}

const styles = StyleSheet.create({
    powderBlueBox: {
        width: Dimensions.get('window').width / 2,
        height: Dimensions.get('window').height / 5,
```

```
        backgroundColor: 'powderblue'
    }
});
```

In the result, we have one working `View` that adapts to a dimension change. It is done using the custom event listener that we registered using React lifecycle methods (`componentWillMount` and `componentWillUnmount`). However, the other, which uses `StyleSheet`, is not adapting. It has no access to `this.state`. StyleSheets are generally meant to be static to provide optimizations such as sending styles only once through the bridge to native.

What if we want our `StyleSheet` styles to adapt anyway? We can do one of the following:

- Resign from StyleSheet and create a custom function that returns an object that represents styles and passes them as inline ones. It will provide similar decoupling if that is the goal:

```
dynamicStyles(newWidth, newHeight) {
    return {
        // calculate styles using passed newWidth, newHeight
    }
}
...
render = () => (
<View
    style={
        this.dynamicStyles(this.state.window.width,
this.state.window.height)
    }
>
...
</View>
)
```

- Use `styles` to override the syntax in the markup:

```
<View
    style={[
        styles.powderBlueBox,
        {
            width: this.state.window.width / 2,
            height: this.state.window.height / 5
        }
    ]}
/>
```

- Use `StyleSheet.flatten` to override `styles` outside of the markup:

```
const powderBlueBox = StyleSheet.flatten([
    styles.powderBlueBox,
    {
        width: this.state.window.width / 4,
        height: this.state.window.height / 5
    }
]);

return (
    ...
        <View style={powderBlueBox} />
    ...
);
```

As with inline styles, beware of the performance implications. You will lose the optimizations when it comes to style-caching. Most likely, on every re-render, `styles` will be recalculated and sent over the bridge again.

Absolute and relative positioning

This section is on the basics of positioning things. In React Native, everything is `relative` by default. This means that if I nest `View` into another `View` that has `marginTop: 40`, this positioning will affect my nested `View` too.

In React Native, we can also change positioning to `absolute`. Then the position will be calculated by a fixed number of pixels from our parent. Use the `top`/`bottom` + `left`/`right` keys in StyleSheet. Remember, other Views will not take this position into account. This is handy if you want to make Views overlap:

Three boxes overlap other because they are absolute-positioned to do so

Check out the following code for the preceding example of three overlapping boxes:

```
// src/ Chapter 3/ Example_6/ App.js

export default () => (
    <View>
        <View style={[styles.box]}>
            <Text style={styles.text}>B1</Text>
        </View>
        <View style={[styles.box, {
            left: 80,
            top: 80,
            backgroundColor: 'steelblue'
        }]}
        >
            <Text style={styles.text}>B2</Text>
        </View>
        <View style={[styles.box, {
            left: 120,
            top: 120,
            backgroundColor: 'powderblue'
        }]}
        >
            <Text style={styles.text}>B3</Text>
        </View>
    </View>
);

const styles = StyleSheet.create({
    box: {
        position: 'absolute',
        top: 40,
        left: 40,
        width: 100,
        height: 100,
        backgroundColor: 'red'
    },
    text: {
        color: '#ffffff',
        fontSize: 80
    }
});
```

Components render according to their order in the markup, so B3 draws over B2, and B2 draws over B1.

If you need to put some of the components on top, use the `zIndex` prop. Check out the documentation for a more detailed explanation: `https://facebook.github.io/react-native/docs/layout-props.html#zindex`.

As we have three `absolute` boxes, let's see what happens if we change `B2` to `relative`:

```
<View style={[styles.box, {
    position: 'relative',
    backgroundColor: 'steelblue'
}]}
>
    <Text style={styles.text}>B2</Text>
</View>
```

Suddenly **B1** disappears:

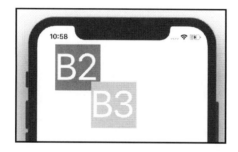

B2 box is now relative to its parent `View`. Hence, its position starts from the upper-left corner of the parent position (as we have no paddings or margins). The **B1** and **B2** boxes are of the same size; **B2** overlaps all of **B1**. If we shrink **B2** a little using `{ width: 50, height: 50 }`, we will see **B1** underneath. I have also changed the font size of the text of **B2** to `40` for clarity. Check out `App.js` in the `src/Chapter 3/Example 7` directory. The results are as follows:

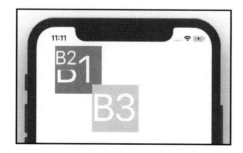

Now that we have learned about absolute and relative positioning, it's time to learn about a great pattern called Flexbox.

Using the Flexible Box pattern

This is one of the greatest patterns that I have learned about when it comes to styling. **Flexible Box (Flexbox)** literally make your boxes flexible.

Let's see a small example. The goal is to flex your box to fill the whole width of the screen:

```
// src/ Chapter_3/ Example_8/ App.js
export default () => (
    <View style={{ flex: 1 }}>
        <View
            style={{ backgroundColor: 'powderblue', height: 50 }}
        />
    </View>
);
```

Here is the result of the preceding code:

Box stretches to the whole screen width because we used flex: 1 styles

It's not too fancy, but you don't need to use `Dimensions`. It is obviously just a start.

You know already that Views are relative to each other by default, so if you want to make some stripes, it's as easy as stacking three `div` on top of each other:

```
// src/ Chapter_3/ Example_8/ App.js

export default () => (
    <View style={{ flex: 1 }}>
        <View
            style={{ backgroundColor: 'powderblue', height: 50 }}
        />
        <View
            style={{ backgroundColor: 'skyblue', height: 50 }}
        />
        <View
```

```
                style={{ backgroundColor: 'steelblue', height: 50 }}
            />
        </View>
    );
```

Check out the following screenshot to see three boxes stretched across the whole screen's width:

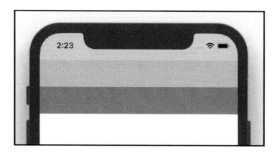

Three boxes in a sequence, each stretched with flex: 1 inherited from parent View component

Now, let's use this fairly easy concept to create header, main content, and footer components. To achieve that, let's flex the middle `View`:

```
<View
    style={{ backgroundColor: 'skyblue', flex: 1 }}
/>
```

Now the middle `View` stretches to fill all available space, leaving 50 dp for the header `View` and another 50 for the footer `View`.

It's time to add some useful content to our divided screen.

In the next sections, I will try to explain Flexbox using examples. But please also check out the Flexbox Froggy game to learn flexbox in different scenarios. It provides an interactive editor and your goal is to move frogs onto the respective leaves `https://github.com/thomaspark/flexboxfroggy/`.

Positioning items with Flexbox

The first important key is `flexDirection`. We can set it to `row`, `row-reverse`, `column`, or `column-reverse`. Flex direction makes content flow in that direction. By default in React Native, flex direction is set to `column`. That's why the boxes in the previous examples are displayed in a column.

Let's use `flexDirection` to display three small sections in the footer: `Home`, `Search`, and `About`:

```
// src / Chapter 3 / Example 9 / App.js
...
<View
    style={{
        backgroundColor: 'steelblue',
        height: 70,
        flexDirection: 'row'
    }}
>
    <View><Text style={{ fontSize: 40 }}>Home</Text></View>
    <View><Text style={{ fontSize: 40 }}>Search</Text></View>
    <View><Text style={{ fontSize: 40 }}>About</Text></View>
</View>
...
```

Okay, we have three separate texts within the footer now. We will learn how to make them switch screens in `Chapters 7`, *Navigation Patterns*.

Our footer looks almost okay:

Three separate footer texts

It's time to learn how to spread views evenly on the x axis. If `flexDirection` is set to `row` or `row-reverse`, we can use `justifyContent`. `justifyContent` accepts the `flex-start`, `flex-end`, `center`, `space-between`, `space-around`, and `space-evenly` values. We will play with them later. For now, let's use `space-between`. It will stretch the `Home` view, the `Search` view, and the `About` view in such a fashion to leave even spaces between them:

```
...
    style={{
        backgroundColor: 'steelblue',
        height: 70,
        justifyContent: 'space-between',
        flexDirection: 'row'
    }}
...
```

The result is as follows:

Three texts in the footer are now separated with even spaces

Although it has nothing to do with flexbox, we can add some padding to make it nicer:

```
paddingLeft: 10,
paddingRight: 10
```

It makes the text easier to read:

Padding on the right and left adds space from the screen edge

What if we want to also position vertically? There is a key for that called `alignItems`. It accepts the `flex-start`, `flex-end`, `center`, `stretch`, and `baseline` values.

Let's now make our footer higher: 100 density-independent pixels. In addition, we want text to be centered vertically:

```
// src / Chapter 3 / Example 10 / App.js
...
    style={{
        backgroundColor: 'steelblue',
        height: 100,
        alignItems: 'center',
        justifyContent: 'space-between',
        flexDirection: 'row',
        paddingLeft: 10,
        paddingRight: 10
    }}
...
```

Check out the result:

Text in the footer is now vertically centered

Styling flex items

As we build the application, you may quickly realize the styles are a little bit ugly. The color palette is a complete disaster. Unless you are a designer, I recommend Googling a color-palette generator. I have changed the colors to be more palatable: white, black, and blue.

Additionally I have added margins and paddings. Everything is nicely separated by a border between the header and content. Let's check out how it looks on the iPhone 8 and iPhone X:

Full application look on iPhone 8 and iPhone X simulators after colour changes

Some of you may not know the basics of styling, so let's quickly explain what margins and paddings are. The **margin** is used to create space around an element. This space is created from the border of the element. You may choose top, bottom, left, or right if you want to apply space only there. The **padding** is very similar, but instead of space outside, it creates space inside. Space is created inside from the border. Check out the element inspector to understand this visually. I have inspected our app header to see how the styles work:

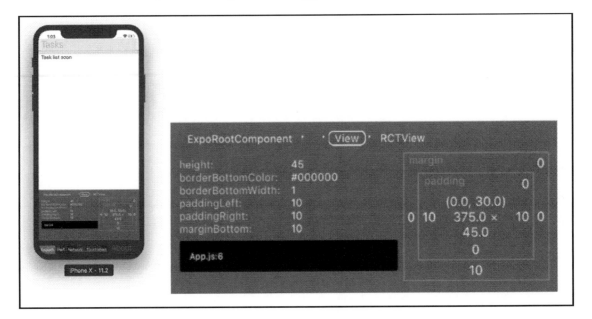

Margin and padding of the Header box

In the previous screenshot, padding is marked with green, and the margin is marked with orange. The component space is light blue. For the exact values specified in styles, please look at the right part of the image.

To open the element inspector, shake your device and, when the menu opens, choose **Toggle element inspector**. If you are using the simulator, you can simulate a shake by choosing the hardware/shake gesture from the simulator menu.

Here are the styles that I used to create `header`:

```
header: {
    height: 45,
    borderBottomColor: '#000000',
    borderBottomWidth: 1,
    paddingLeft: 10,
    paddingRight: 10,
    marginBottom: 10
},
// All the other styles are available in
// src/ Chapter_3/ Example_11/ App.js
```

Next, let's make the footer more reusable. What if, at some point, we don't need the **About** link but a Notifications link instead? This word is really long. It will not fit into our design. While this is a problem now, if we plan to add translations, we will run into this issue there too.

Most applications fix these issues using icons. Let's try that:

1. Install the icon package:

   yarn add @expo/vector-icons

2. Change the footer markup:

   ```
   // src/ Chapter_3/ Example_11/ App.js
   <View style={styles.footer}>
       <Ionicons name="md-home" size={32} color="white" />
       <Ionicons name="md-search" size={32} color="white" />
       <Ionicons name="md-notifications" size={32} color="white" />
   </View>
   ```

The added icons can be observed on the following screenshot:

Application's footer is now made of icons

The footer is now reusable and supports any language. Check what icons mean in other countries if you support their language.

Styling content

We have the footer positioned using the direction row. It's time to position the main content and column. In the previous chapters, we created a task list. This is the time to integrate it with our design.

Add the `TaskList` component into the content box. I also add the `ScrollView` component to make content scrollable in case tasks take up too much space to display all of them:

```
import data from './tasks.json';

// ... header
<ScrollView style={styles.content}>
    <TaskList tasks={data.tasks} />
</ScrollView>
// ... footer
```

My tasks mock in the JSON file is presented as follows. Later on in this book, we will learn how to fetch tasks from a backend server and how to separate such logic from the markup:

```
{
  "tasks": [
    {
      "name": "Task 1",
      "description": "Task 1 description...",
      "likes": 239
    },
    //... more comma separated tasks here
  ]
}
```

Having the mock, we can implement the `TaskList` view:

```
const TaskList = ({ tasks }) => (
    <View>
        {tasks.map(task => (
            <View key={task.name}>
                <Text>{task.name}</Text>
                <Text>{task.description}</Text>
                <LikeCounter likes={task.likes} />
            </View>
        ))}
    </View>
);
// separate component for each task is not created for book clarity
```

LikeCounter is copy-pasted from Chapter 2 / Example 8 / src and tweaked to accept likes as props (replaces the default zero). Please note that it uses Flexbox too, and that flexDirection there is set to row.

Now, we are ready to style the content. Here is our starting point:

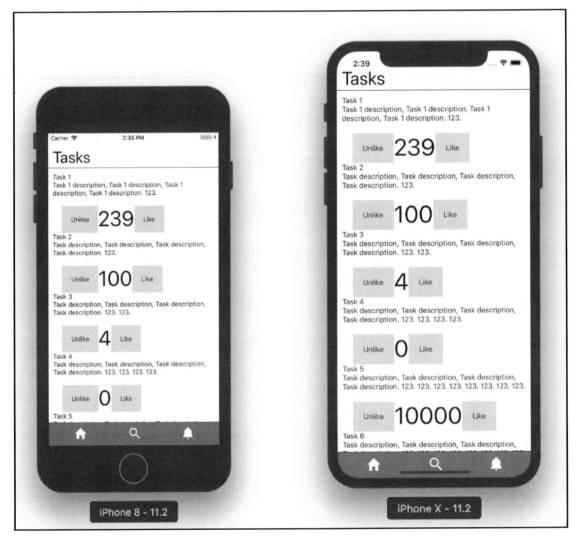

Current look at iPhone 8 and iPhone X simulators

We want to reorganize the contents of each task. The **Like** and **Unlike** widget should be displayed on the right side of the task and should use icons. The task name should be slightly bigger than the description and should fit on 70% of the task width. The right-hand side, with the like/dislike widget, should be separated by a thin grey border. The border should also separate tasks. Add nice paddings and margins where necessary:

Desired look of iPhone 8 and iPhone X simulators

Okay, how do we start? We need to break things up into small pieces that can be implemented separately. Create the following:

- A task `View` with the task-container styling and top-border styling.
- The two inner `Views` – one for the name and description and another for the like counter. These should be displayed in a row.
- The name and description `View` should have two `Views` inside: one for the name and one for the description. Add styling to make `fontSize` bigger for name.
- The like counter `View` container should define the border on the left. The container should have two `Views` inside: one for the number of likes and another for the like/dislike icons. These `Views` should use column as the default direction.
- The View with the like/dislike icons should have row direction flexbox styling.

As we have that, use `alignItems` and `justifyContent` to position elements vertically or horizontally. Please look at helper images from the inspector:

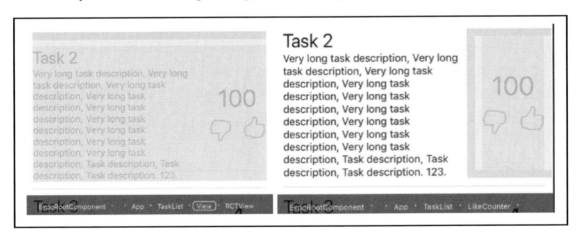

Inspector view of implemented components. Serves as a hint for implementation.

The orange highlight represents the `View` margin, and the green highlight represents the `View` padding.

Try implementing this yourself. The full solution is available in the `src/ Chapter_3/ Example_12/ src/` folder, in the `App.js`, `TaskList.js`, and `LikeCounter.js` files.

Solving the text overflow problem

One of the most common problems is text overflow. The easiest trick to solve this is to wrap text, but sometimes it is not possible. Examples:

- Button text
- Large number that needs to be displayed (for instance, the like count)
- Long word that should not be broken down

The question is: how can we approach this problem? There are many solutions. Let's look at a few.

Scaling the font down

This is possible on iOS right now:

```
<Text
    style={styles.text}
    numberOfLines={1}
    adjustsFontSizeToFit
>
    {this.state.likeCount}
</Text>
```

But, the outcome is a complete disaster in our case. The layout feels very inconsistent, even if we put some work into this scaling solution:

Automatic font adjustment using the adjustsFontSizeToFit prop for iOS

As shown earlier in the book, you could use `Dimensions` instead of relying on `adjustsFontSizeToFit`. Based on `Dimensions`, you can create a scaling function to compute `fontSize`.

Truncating text

Another approach is known as **truncating**. Based on the text length, you cut it at some point and add three dots instead, ... However, this approach is not good for our use case. We work with the likes count number and we want to know what the number is:

```
<Text style={styles.text}>
    {
        this.state.likeCount.toString().length > 4
            ? `${this.state.likeCount.toString().substring(0, 4)}...`
            : this.state.likeCount
    }
</Text>
```

Observe the truncated number of likes in the following screenshot:

Truncated numbers are meaningless, this solution works only for text

Using the Kilo social media notation

You know that kilo means 1,000. Social media designers pushed this idea to the web and mobiles. Whenever a number is greater than 1,000, they replace the last 3 digits with K. For instance 20K means 20,000.

The trivial implementation:

```
const likes = this.state.likeCount.toString();
...
<Text style={styles.text}>
    {
        likes.length > 3
            ? `${likes.substring(0, likes.length - 3)}K`
            : likes
    }
</Text>
```

However, a number such as *9,876,543,210* is going to overflow again. But 9,876,543K is still too long. Let's solve this with a simple recursive function:

```
// src / Chapter 3 / Example 12 / src / LikeCounter.js

kiloText = (nr, nrK = 0) => (nr.length > 3
    ? this.kiloText(nr.substring(0, nr.length - 3), nrK + 1)
    : nr + Array(nrK).fill('K').join(''))
```

This algorithm works as follows:
The function takes a number in a string format and an optional parameter that indicates how many thousands are already stripped of the original number.

It checks whether it can strip another thousand, if so, it returns the outcome of itself with the number stripped by three numbers and the number of thousands increased by one.

If the number length is less than four, compute the text: take the number and attach the relevant number of Ks as the suffix. We compute Ks using a neat trick: create an array of size equal to the number of Ks, fill every element with the K string, and join all the elements into one long string.

The JSX is now much simpler:

```
<Text style={styles.text}>
    {this.kiloText(likes)}
</Text>
```

Check the result is as follows. The long number is now shown using the kilo notation:

A big like count is now displayed using the kilo (K) notation

It is a safe bet that the number of likes will not exceed 9,000,000,000. If you need to support larger numbers, try the **M** or **B** letters.

React Native animated

As we build our application, we need to focus on the **user experience (UX)**. One part of it is animations that make our screens more vibrant and provide instant feedback on the actions. If you played with our application on your own, you could see that when you click the like/dislike icon, it makes a little blink. That effect comes out of the box with `TouchableOpacity`. It's time to learn how we can implement such features on our own.

What are animations?

When I first read the Animated library documentation I freaked out. There are so many new words that you will need to get used to. Instead of diving right into them, let's understand what animations really are.

Animation is a change to a component style over time.

 Remember: you need a style attribute, its starting value, and its end value. Animation is what you see when this value goes from start to end over time. You can combine many attributes and possibly animate many components at the same time.

The common and recommended way to store variables that will change over time is the component state. React Native Animated provides a special class that implements this functionality in a very performant way: `Animated.Value`. For example:

```
state = {
    fadeIn: new Animated.Value(0)
}
```

Changing attributes over time

In React Native, there are three main ways to create animations:

- `Animated.timing()`: Takes time in milliseconds and desired end value, and maps them to your `Animated.Value`.
- `Animated.decay()`: Starts with an initial velocity and slowly decays.
- `Animated.spring()`: Provides a simple spring physics model.

Let's see how it works in action. Our goal will be to fade in application on the app's start. To achieve a fade-in effect, we will manipulate opacity from 0 to 1. The animation should take two seconds:

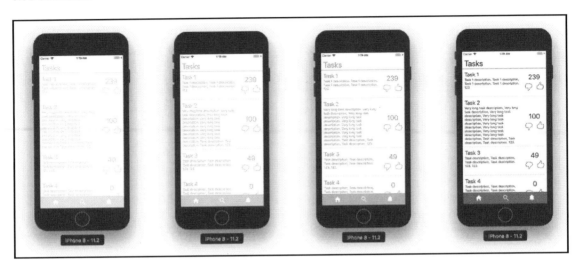

Sequence of images showing the opacity animation progress over time

`Animated.timing` expects two arguments: variable to be manipulated and config object. In a config object, you need to specify the `toValue` key to tell the function what should be the end value of your variable after the duration of milliseconds – in our case, 2,000. I chose two seconds just for the animation to be a little easier to see. Play around with it:

```
// src/ Chapter_3/ Example_13/ src/ App.js
class App extends React.Component {
    state = {
        fadeIn: new Animated.Value(0)
    }

    componentDidMount() {
        this.fadeInApp();
    }

    fadeInApp() {
        Animated.timing(
            this.state.fadeIn,
            {
                toValue: 1,
                duration: 2000,
```

```
                    easing: Easing.linear
            }
        ).start();
    }

    render = () => (
        <Animated.View
            style={[
                styles.appContainer,
                { opacity: this.state.fadeIn }
            ]}
        >
            ... // rest of render removed for clarity
        </Animated.View>
    )
}
```

We have also introduced a new component: `Animated.View`. It makes our usual `View` component support animations.

React Native Animated provides animatable components: `Animated.Image`, `Animated.ScrollView`, `Animated.Text`, and `Animated.View`, but you can also define your own using the `createAnimatedComponent()` function.

Additionally, in the config object, we specified **easing**. Easing is how the animation should go. If it should change the value linearly over time then use `Easing.linear`. Linear however is not natural. Check the next section to learn more about easing functions.

 Learning animations takes time. You can create countless different scenarios and you should play around with the API on your own. Especially when it comes to `Animated.decay` and `Animated.spring`. I'm not covering them in the book as it is not a very big pattern, it is just another API you need to learn. In the next sections, we will focus on ways to chain animations and then how to make them performant.

Think about how to create a draggable box using `Animated.decay`. You will also need a `PanResponder` component. On the release of a touch event, it should maintain its speed in the same direction and should slowly stop after flying some distance.
The second exercise could be implementing a red square box with a button underneath. On a button press, the square box should expand its width and height by another 15 density-independent pixels. All should be done with a spring animation, thus width should go a little beyond 15 and then go back to 15. Just like a spring does.

If these two exercises sound tough, please proceed to the next section. They should get easier once you learn about easing functions.

The easing function

An animation is a change over time. This change can be applied in many ways. The function that determines the new value over time is known as an easing function.

Why do we use easing functions instead of linear easing? The common example I like is a drawer opening. When you open a drawer in the real world, is it a linear process? Perhaps not.

Now let's look at the common easing functions. There are a few. Choose the one that fits your application:

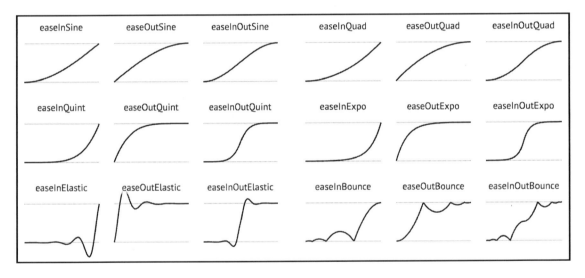

Many different easing functions with a visualization of each one changes value over time.

On the graphs, grey lines indicate the start and end value. The black line represents how the value changes over time. Eventually, the black line reaches the upper grey line. As you can see, some easing functions go below the start value or beyond the end value. Those may be useful for highlighting important actions.

Want to see more easing functions? Check out http://easings.net/. Most of these functions can be implemented using the RN Easing module.

Back to React Native easings. I have prepared an application for you to play around with easing functions. You will find the source code at src/ Chapter_3/ Example_14/ App.js:

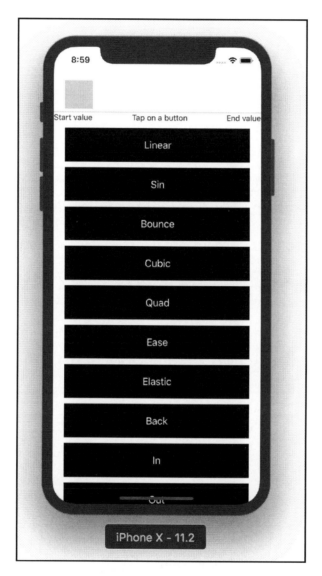

Easing functions playground application

When you click on a button, you will see a box moving from left to right with the respective easing function.

As for the animation, I do it by manipulating `marginLeft` of the box. The animation starts with `marginLeft` set to 20 and applies the easing function to reach 300 over 2 seconds:

```
// src/ Chapter_3/ Example_14/ App.js
// ...
animate(easing) {
    this.easeValue.setValue(20);
    Animated.timing(
        this.easeValue,
        {
            toValue: 300,
            duration: 2000,
            easing
        }
    ).start();
}

onPress = easingName => this.animate(Easing[easingName.toLowerCase()]);
// ...
```

Scheduling events

As we know how to create animations, now let's talk about how to schedule them.

The trivial approach is a delayed animation dispatch:

- `Animated.delay()`: Starts an animation after a given delay. Good if you need to delay your response to a user action. But usually this is not a case.

Let's talk about array of events that we want to schedule. More than one event should be dispatched. If we need all of the events to happen at the same time, it is also trivial:

- `Animated.parallel()`: Starts a number of animations at the same time. But what if we need to time them one after another? Here comes sequence.

- `Animated.sequence()`: Starts the animations in order, waiting for each one to complete before starting the next. There is also a variation of parallel. It is called stagger.

- `Animated.stagger()`: Starts animations in order and in parallel, but with successive delays.

Exercise time: Fill the screen with rows of colored boxes. Rows should appear on the screen one after another in a staggered fashion:

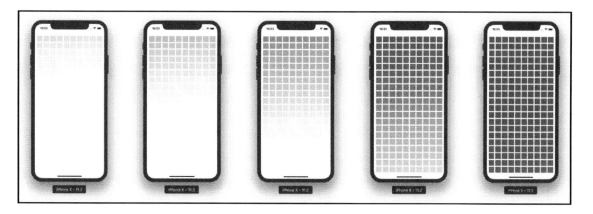

Images showing the stagger animation over time

The full implementation is available at `src/ Chapter_3/ Example_15/ App.js.` Let's look at a key fragment:

```
// ...
getFadeInAnimation = animatedVal =>
    Animated.timing(animatedVal, { toValue: 1, duration: 5000 });

componentDidMount() {
    const animations = Boxes.map(box =>
        this.getFadeInAnimation(this.state[box]));
    Animated.stagger(10, animations).start();
}
// ...
```

The first function is just a helper. It generates one timed animation. We use this helper function to generate all the animations and collect them in the `animations` variable. The helper function expects `animatedVal`, which will be eased to 1. In my implementation, I have created a separate `Animated.Value` in the state for each of the boxes. In the end, I pass a generated array of animations to stagger and immediately start.

Pretty nice animation, right? Now, let's talk about performance.

Measuring FPS

Websites and mobile applications use animations pretty rarely. Most of the time, it's in response to user actions that tend to be slow. If you've ever played a dynamic computer game, you probably remember what a different world it is. Yes, as we dive into animations, there is one thing from computer games that you should remember: **FPS**.

Frames per second – everything on the screen appears in motion thanks to the optical illusion created by quickly changing frames at a consistent speed. 60 FPS means 60 frames per second, which means you see a new frame every 16.67ms. JavaScript needs to deliver that frame in this short period, otherwise the frame will be dropped. If so, your FPS metric will drop below 60.

React Native is known for its amazing performance in most of the applications: **60 FPS**. But, as we start using a lot of animations, we can quickly kill that performance. In this section, I want to show you how to measure FPS in your application.

Let's check how well we do with our previous animation:

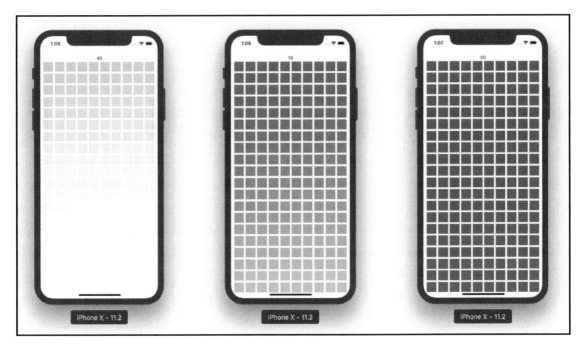

Images showing the stagger animation over time

We will measure this animation. On a simulator, I get **48** FPS with animations halfway started. Near the finish, FPS drops down to **18**. When all animations complete, FPS is back to its normal 60. I have also checked on my real phone (iPhone 7 plus) and the results were similar.

This is just an example of the FPS drop in the development environment. However, you should test your application on real production builds instead. Learn more at `https://facebook.github.io/react-native/docs/performance.html`.

How to measure FPS

It's time to learn how to check FPS. There are two main ways:

- Use a tool, such as Perf Monitor. It provides this functionality out of the box. It allows you to also measure the native environment.
- Write custom JavaScript code to measure FPS. This will only measure the JS thread's performance.

Using a performance monitor with the *Create React Native* App is as easy as shaking your device and choosing the **Show Perf Monitor** option:

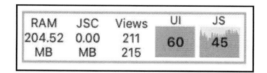

Show perf monitor. Numbers 60 and 45 represent the latest value of the FPS measure

Implementing your own solution in JavaScript should rely on the fact that a desired 60FPS mean a frame every 16.67ms (1000ms/60). I have created a simple example for you:

```
// src / Chapter 3 / Example 16 / App.js
constructor() {
    // ...
    let FPScounter = 0;
    setInterval(() => FPScounter++, 16);
    setInterval(() => {
        this.setState({ fps: FPScounter });
        FPScounter = 0;
    }, 1000);
}
// ...
render = () => (
    // ...
    <Text>FPS: {this.state.fps}</Text>
    // ...
);
// makes sure these measures are only done in dev environment
```

```
// and never leak to the production app!
// Beware: This example is not really very accurate and performant
// I have made it to illustrate the idea
```

As this book strives to teach you design patterns, I hope you will also check whether your solutions are performant.

Summary

In this chapter, you learned how to style React Native applications. We introduced many different ways of positioning elements and you learned how our designs translate to real devices. In the end, we made a few animations and measured them in terms of FPS.

So far, we know how to create reusable code using React components and how to style them. We worked with limited data stored in the local JSON file. It's time to make our application more complex and talk about different scenarios that impact big applications. In the next chapter, you will learn about Flux, which is an architectural pattern.

4
Flux Architecture

If you have used React before, you may have heard of Flux already. If not, don't worry. Flux is an architectural pattern for building React user interfaces. We will start off with the one-direction dataflow pattern that React uses and that will lead us on to Flux. Every bit that makes Flux tick is important and I highly recommend you spend some time on this chapter. The minimum two points you should take away are how to separate the code and how to split an application into parts using Flux. Those small services connected together are responsible for everything that a modern mobile application needs.

One-direction dataflow pattern

Before we dive into the Flux architecture, let's look at the historical background for this pattern. I want you to understand why it was introduced.

Watching Facebook developers talking about the Flux architecture, I had a gut feeling that they switched to Flux from the **Model-View-Controller** (**MVC**) pattern. The MVC pattern the decoupling of your business model from view markup and coded logic. Logic is encapsulated by a function called a controller and it delegates work to services. Hence, we say we aim for lean controllers.

However, at a larger scale, such as that seen at Facebook, it looks like this pattern is not enough. As it allows bidirectional dataflow, it quickly becomes hard to understand and even harder to track. One change caused by an event can loop back and cascade the effect throughout the application. Imagine if you had to find a bug in such an architecture.

React's one-way data binding

React's solution for the preceding problem starts with one-way data binding. This means that the view layer is maintained by a component and only the component can update the view. The resulting native code is computed by the component's render function and displayed to the end user. If the view layer needs to respond to the user's actions, it can only dispatch events that are handled by the component. It cannot directly change **state** or **props**.

Let's look at the following diagram, which illustrates this concept:

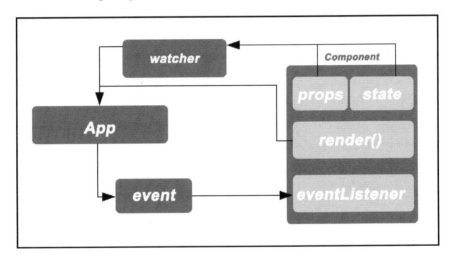

The **App** block represents the state of the native view layer. In the diagram, the components are simplified to: props, state, the render function, and event listeners. Once anything changes in props or state, the watcher calls the render function to update the native view. Once the user performs an action, a respective event is dispatched and then picked up by event listeners.

In the two-way data binding schema, the **App** layer does not need to dispatch an event. It can directly modify the state of the component. We can simulate this with event listeners too. One example of this is controlled input, which we learned about in Chapter 2, *View Patterns*.

Event problems

"With great freedom comes great responsibility."

You have probably heard this saying already. This sentiment applies to events that we dispatch and handle. Let's discuss some of the issues.

First of all, to listen to an event, you need to create an event listener. When should it be created? Usually, we create event listeners in a component with markup and register using `onClick={this.someEventListener}`. What if this event needs to cause a change to a completely different component? In this case, we need to lift the listener up the component tree into some container.

As we do this, we notice that we couple more and more components more tightly, passing increasing numbers of listeners down the prop chain. This is a nightmare we want to avoid, if possible.

 Hence, Flux introduces the concept of the Dispatcher. The Dispatcher sends an event to all of the registered components. This way, every component can react to events related to it, while ignoring the unrelated events. We will discuss this concept later on in this chapter.

Further issues with binding

Using one-way data binding is not enough, as you can see. We can quickly fall into traps that simulate two-way data binding, or run into problems with events, as mentioned in the previous section.

Everything comes down to the question: can we handle it? For large scale applications, the answer is usually *no*. We need a predictable model that guarantees that we can find out quickly what happened and why. If the events are occurring all over our application, the developer will obviously have to spend a lot of time finding out what specifically is causing the detected bug.

How can we narrow down this problem? The answer is restrictions. We need some restrictions on the event flow. This is where the Flux architecture kicks in.

Introduction to Flux

The Flux architecture creates some restrictions on communication between components. The main principle is that of ubiquitous actions. The application view layer responds to user actions by sending action objects to a Dispatcher. The Dispatcher's role is to send every action to subscribed **stores**. You can have many stores and each one can act differently in response to the user's action.

For instance, imagine you are building a cart-based application. A user can tap the screen to add some item to the cart, upon which the respective action is dispatched and your cart store reacts to it. Also, an analytics store may track that such an item has been added to the user's cart. Both react to the same action object and use the information as needed. In the end, the view layer is updated with the new state.

Replacing MVC

In order to enhance MVC architecture, let's remind ourselves of how it looks:

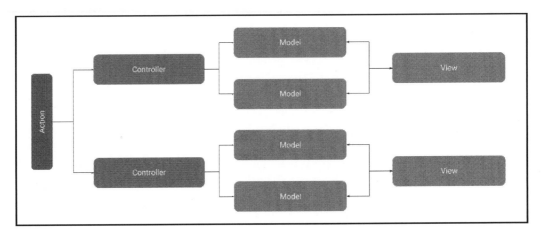

Actions are handled by their respective controllers, which have access to models (data representations). View is usually coupled to the model and may update it as needed.

When I was reading this architecture for the first time, I struggled to understand it. Let me give you some tips if you haven't work with it yourself yet:

- Action: Think of this as a user's action, such as a button tap, scroll, and navigation change.
- Controller: This is the piece responsible for handling the action and displaying the appropriate native view.
- Model: This is a data structure that holds information separated from the view. The view needs a model to display it visually according to the design.
- View: This is what the end user sees. The view describes all markup code, which can later on be styled. The view is sometimes coupled to styles and referred to as one piece.

As the application grows, the little architecture sooner or later becomes something like the following:

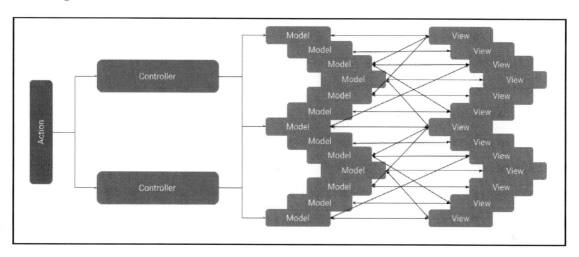

In this diagram, I tried to show that some models rely on others by creating an indentation in the structure of the models. It is a similar case for views. This should not be considered bad. Generally, this architecture works to some extent. Problems arise when you identify a bug and find yourself unable to locate where and why something is going wrong. To be more precise, you lose control over the flow of information. You find yourself in a spot where so many things are happening at the same moment that you cannot easily predict what is responsible for the failure, nor why it is happening. Sometimes, you even struggle to reproduce the bug or validate if it is, in fact, a bug.

Looking at the diagram, you can spot an issue in model-view communication: it goes in both directions. This is what software has been doing for years. Some brilliant mind realized that in a client environment, we can afford one-direction dataflow. That will effectively make the architecture predictable. If our controllers only had a series of input data, and were then supposed to deliver a new state of the view, it would feel much clearer. Unit tests could provide series of data, such as an input, and assert on an output. Similarly, a tracking service could record any errors and save the input data series.

Let's look at the dataflow Flux proposes:

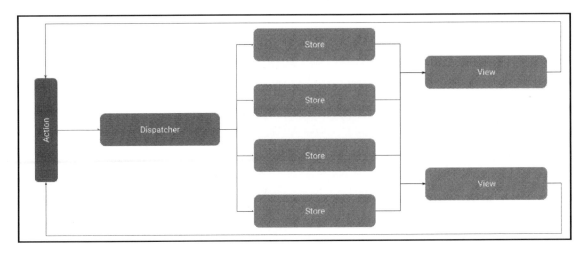

All actions go through the Dispatcher and are then sent to registered store callbacks. In the end, the store contents are mapped to a view.

This can get complicated with time, as can be seen in the following diagram:

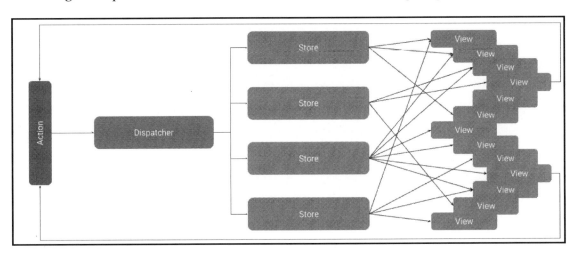

You are likely to have a variety of stores that are used on different views or view partials. Our views are composed into one final view that the user sees. If something changes, another action is dispatched into the stores. These stores calculate a new state and refresh the views.

This is much simpler. We can now track actions and see which action led to unwanted changes in the stores.

Flux by example

Before we dive in-depth into Flux, let's create a simple application using the Flux architecture. For this, we will use the Flux library provided by Facebook. The library includes all of the pieces we will need to make the application tick according to the new Flux flow. Install Flux and the `immutable` libraries. `immutable` is also crucial for further advantages as we become more familiar with Flux:

```
yarn add flux immutable
```

The application we will build in Flux is a Tasks application. The one we have already created will need some tweaking. The first thing to do is create the `Dispatcher`, Tasks Store, and Task Actions.

The Flux package provides the base for our architecture. For instance, let's instantiate `Dispatcher` for our Tasks application:

```
// src / Chapter 4_ Flux patterns / Example 1 / src / data /
AppDispatcher.js
import { Dispatcher } from 'flux';

export default new Dispatcher();
```

`Dispatcher` will be used to dispatch actions, but we need to create the actions first. I will follow the documentation advice and create action types as the first step:

```
// src / Chapter 4_ Flux patterns / Example 1 / src / data /
TasksActionTypes.js
const ActionTypes = {
    ADD_TASK: 'ADD_TASK'
};

export default ActionTypes;
```

Now that we have created the types, we should follow up with the action creator itself, as seen here:

```
// src / Chapter 4_ Flux patterns / Example 1 / src / data / TaskActions.js
import TasksActionTypes from './TasksActionTypes';
import AppDispatcher from './AppDispatcher';
```

```
const Actions = {
    addTask(task) {
        AppDispatcher.dispatch({
            type: TasksActionTypes.ADD_TASK,
            task
        });
    }
};

export default Actions;
```

So far, we have actions and a tool to dispatch them. The missing piece is the Store, which will react to actions. Let's create TodoStore:

```
// src / Chapter 4_ Flux patterns / Example 1 / src / data / TaskStore.js
import Immutable from 'immutable';
import { ReduceStore } from 'flux/utils';
import TasksActionTypes from './TasksActionTypes';
import AppDispatcher from './AppDispatcher';

class TaskStore extends ReduceStore {
    constructor() {
        super(AppDispatcher);
    }

    getInitialState() {
        return Immutable.List([]);
    }

    reduce(state, action) {
        switch (action.type) {
        case TasksActionTypes.ADD_TASK:
            return state; // <= placeholder, to be replaced!!!
        default:
            return state;
        }
    }
}

export default new TaskStore();
```

To create the Store, we import `ReduceStore` from `flux/utils`. The store class should be extended to provide the necessary API methods. We will cover these in a later section. As for now, you should have spotted that you need to pass `Dispatcher` to the upper class using `super` in the constructor.

Separately, let's implement the `reduce` case for `ADD_TASK`. The same flow can be tweaked to any other action type you want to create:

```
reduce(state, action) {
    switch (action.type) {
    case TasksActionTypes.ADD_TASK:
        if (!action.task.name) {
            return state;
        }
        return state.push({
            name: action.task.name,
            description: action.task.description,
            likes: 0
        });
    default:
        return state;
    }
}
```

As we now have all of the bits for the Flux architecture (`Action`, `Dispatcher`, `Store`, and `View`), we can connect all of them together. For this, flux/utils exposes a handy container factory method. Please note that I will reuse view from our previous Task application. I have removed the likes counter for clarity:

```
// src / Chapter 4 / Example 1 / src / App.js
import { Container } from 'flux/utils';
import TaskStore from './data/TaskStore';
import AppView from './views/AppView';

const getStores = () => [TaskStore];
const getState = () => ({ tasks: TaskStore.getState() });

export default Container.createFunctional(AppView, getStores, getState);
```

If you have not followed this book from the start, please note that we are using container component here. This pattern is fairly important to understand and we went through it in Chapter 1, *React Component Patterns*. There, you can learn how to create container components from scratch.

Our application is now equipped with the Flux architecture tools. The last thing we need to do is refactor to follow our new principles.

To do this, these are our tasks:

1. Initialize store with tasks, instead of passing JSON data directly to the view.
2. Create an add task form that dispatches an ADD_TASK action on submit.

The first one is fairly simple:

```
// src / Chapter 4_ Flux patterns / Example 1 / src / data / TaskStore.js
import data from './tasks.json';

class TaskStore extends ReduceStore {
// ...
    getInitialState() {
        return Immutable.List([...data.tasks]);
    }
// ...
```

The second one requires us to use the Input component. Let's create a separate file that is responsible for the whole feature. In this file, we will create states for name and description, a handleSubmit function that dispatches the ADD_TASK action, and a render function with the form view markup:

```
// src / Chapter 4_ Flux patterns / Example 1 / src / views /
AddTaskForm.js

export const INITIAL_ADD_TASK_FORM_STATE = {
    name: '',
    description: ''
};

class AddTaskForm extends React.Component {
    constructor(props) {
        super(props);
        this.handleSubmit.bind(this);
    }
```

```
    state = INITIAL_ADD_TASK_FORM_STATE;

    handleSubmit = () => {
        TaskActions.addTask({
            name: this.state.name,
            description: this.state.description
        });
        this.setState(INITIAL_ADD_TASK_FORM_STATE);
    };

    render = () => (
        <View style={styles.container}>
            <TextInput
                style={styles.input}
                placeholder="Name"
                onChangeText={name => this.setState({ name })}
                value={this.state.name}
            />
            <TextInput
                style={styles.input}
                placeholder="Description"
                onChangeText={d => this.setState({ description: d })}
                value={this.state.description}
            />
            <Button
                title="Add task"
                onPress={() => this.handleSubmit()}
            />
        </View>
    );
}

// ... styles
```

The fully functional app will look as follows:

Now that we have created our first app that follows the Flux architecture, it's time to deep dive into the API.

Detailed Flux diagram

Let's look at the Flux architecture in a more formalized way. Here is a little diagram that shows how the simplified architecture looks:

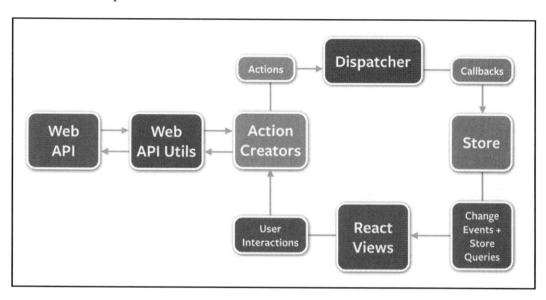

Flux diagram from official documentation: https://github.com/facebook/flux

Each of the pieces in the preceding diagram has its own purpose in the circular chain:

- Dispatcher: The manager of what's happening in the application. This manages actions and provides them to registered callbacks. All actions need to pass through the Dispatcher. The Dispatcher must expose the `register` and `unregister` methods to register/unregister callbacks, and must expose the `dispatch` method, which dispatches actions.

- Stores: The application consists of multiple stores that register callback(s) in the Dispatcher. Each store needs to expose a public `constructor` method that accepts the `Dispatcher` argument. The constructor is responsible for registering this store instance with the given Dispatcher.

- React views: This topic was covered in the previous chapter. Please have a look if you have not followed this book from the beginning.

- Action creators: These compose data into an action object that is delivered to the Dispatcher. This process may involve data fetching and other means to obtain the necessary data. , action creators may lead to **side effects**. We will cover this topic in the next section. The action creator must return a plain action object at the end.

You can find the full API reference for each piece under the following link: https://facebook.github.io/flux/.

What are side effects?

A side effect is an application state change that happens outside of the called function—to be precise, any state change other than its return value.

Here are some examples of side effects:

- Modifying a global variable
- Modifying a variable in a parent scope chain
- Writing to the screen
- Writing to the file
- Any network request, for instance, an AJAX request

This section on side effects is meant to get you ready for the next chapter, where we will talk about pure functions in the context of Redux. Also, we will push these ideas much further in `Chapter 9`, *Functional Programming Patterns*, where you will learn how we can benefit from functional programming practices, such as mutable and `immutable` objects, higher order functions, and monads.

Why recognize side effects?

Side effects manipulate the state that is not the property of the function. Hence, when we look at the function in isolation, it is hard to assess whether the function has any negative implications on the application. This is not only true in unit tests; it is also cumbersome when it comes to mathematical proofs. Some big applications that must be secure can strive to build a mathematical model that is bullet-proof. Such apps are proved using math tools that go beyond the material of this book.

Side effects, when isolated, may work as data providers to our app. They can "inject" into the flow at the best moment, and from then on, data is treated as if it was just a variable. Going from one side effect free, function to another. Such a side effect-free function chain is easier to debug, and in some cases, replay. By replay, I mean passing the exact same input data to assess the output and see it if meets business criteria.

Let's look at the practical side of this concept from the perspectives of both MVC and Flux.

Working with side effects in MVC

If we follow classic MVC architecture, we will work with separation of concerns as follows: model, view, and controller. Also, the view may get exposed functions that directly update the model. If this happens, it may trigger side effects.

There are a couple of places where side effects could be placed:

- Controller initialization
- Controller-related service (this service is a decoupled specialized piece of logic)
- The view, using the controller-related service exposed as a callback
- In some cases, on model update (server-client bidirectional model)

I'm sure you can even come up with more than that.

This freedom comes at a great cost. We can have virtually unlimited numbers of paths intertwined with side effects, as follows:

- Side effect => Controller => Model => View
- Controller => Side effect => Model => View
- Controller => View => Model => Side effect

This kills our ability to reason, in a functional side effect-free way, on the application as a whole.

How does MVC usually handle this issue? The answer is simple—most of the time this architecture does not care about it. As long as we could assert the app is working as expected by unit tests, we would be happy enough.

But then Facebook came along and claimed that we can do it better on the frontend side. Thanks to the specific nature of the frontend, we can be more organized and opinionated on the flow, without significant performance loss.

Working with side effects in Flux

In Flux, we still retain the freedom to choose the place where side effects are triggered, but we must respect unidirectional flow.

Some examples of possible side effects in Flux include the following:

- Downloading data on user click and then sending it to the Dispatcher
- The Dispatcher downloads data before sending data to registered callbacks
- The store commences synchronous side effects to retain necessary data for update

A good idea is to force side effects to occur in only one place in the Flux architecture. We could perform side effects only on action triggers. For instance, when the SHOW_MORE action is triggered by a user click, we first download the data and then send the full object to the Dispatcher. Hence, neither the Dispatcher nor any store need to perform side effects. This nice idea is used in **Redux Thunk.** We will learn about Redux and Redux Thunk in the next chapter.

Side effects are crucial in understanding the more advanced material in this book. As we have now learned about side effects, let's proceed to the chapter summary.

Summary

To sum up, Flux is a very good invention for large-scale applications. It solves problems where the classic MVC pattern struggles to do so. Events are unidirectional, which makes communication more predictable. The domain of your application can easily be mapped to stores and then maintained with a domain expert.

All of these things are available thanks to a well-thought-out pattern consisting of a Dispatcher, stores, and actions. In this chapter, we made our little Flux-based application using flux-utils, Facebook's official library.

Having connected all of these pieces, we are ready to deep-dive into one particular aspect—stores. There are a few patterns that you can use to put your store on another level. One of these is Redux library. We will explore the different capabilities that Redux provides in the next chapter.

Questions

1. Why did Facebook move away from the classic MVC architecture?
   Answer: Facebook identified issues with MVC experienced when working with the kind of large scale necessary for Facebook. In the frontend application, views and models were tightly coupled. Bidirectional dataflow made it even worse: it was hard to debug how the data transitioned between models and views and which parts were responsible for the end state.
2. What are the main benefits of Flux's architecture?
   Answer: Watch the video **Hacker Way: Rethinking Web App Development at Facebook** mentioned in the *Further reading* section or see the section on *Replacing MVC*.
3. Can you draw a diagram of the Flux architecture? Can you do it in detailed way with web APIs drawn and connected to your diagram?
   Answer: Check *Detailed flux diagram* section.
4. What is the role of the Dispatcher?
   Answer: Check *Flux introduction* or *Detailed flux diagram* if you need to go over the full explanation again.
5. Can you give four examples of side effects?
   Answer: Check *Flux introduction*.
6. How can side effects be decoupled in Flux architecture?
   Answer: Check the section on *Working with side effects in Flux*.

Further reading

- The official Flux documentation page can be found at `https://facebook.github.io/flux/`.
- Flux examples from the GitHub repository can be found at `https://github.com/facebook/flux/tree/master/examples`.
- The Facebook conference video (F8 2014) called **Hacker Way: Rethinking Web App Development at Facebook** is available at `https://www.youtube.com/watch?v=nYkdrAPrdcw`.
- **Flux in React Native - Yoav Amit**, Wix Engineering Tech Talks is available at `https://www.youtube.com/watch?v=m-rMK5ZZM5k`.

5
Store Patterns

The patterns built around virtual stores in JavaScript contain everything that is needed to decide what to show in an application. In my opinion, it is the most important piece necessary to understand Flux well, hence, I have dedicated a special chapter to store patterns, to go through many examples and compare alternatives. As React Native applications usually need to work offline, we will also learn how to transition our JavaScript store into a persistent store on a user's mobile device. This will take our application to the next level when it comes to user experience.

In this chapter, you will learn the following:

- How to integrate Redux into your Flux architecture
- How Redux differs from classic Flux and the benefits of the new approach
- The core principles of Redux
- How to create a store that will be a single source of truth
- What effect patterns and side effects are

Using Redux stores

It took me a while to figure out how to advertise Redux to you. Most likely, you expect it is some sort of Store implementation that will be used within Flux. This is true; however, there is more to it than that. Redux is a brilliant piece of code that makes a great tool. This tool can be used in many ways in many different projects. In this book, I strive to teach you to think in React and Redux.

This introduction was inspired by a useful talk from Cheng Lou, called *Taming the Meta Language*, and delivered at React Conf 2017.
Watch it at `https://goo.gl/2SkWAj`.

Minimal Redux application example

Before I show you the Redux architecture, let's see it in action. It is vital to get a feeling for what the Redux API looks like. Once we develop the simplest hello world app in Redux, we will move on to a more high-level overview.

The hello world app we will be building is a counter app, as simple as two buttons (increase and decrease) and a text indicating the current count.

Before we dive in, let's install two packages using the following command:

```
yarn add redux react-redux
```

Okay, first, let's create some basic Flux pieces that we already know, but this time using the Redux API:

- ActionTypes:

    ```
    // Chapter 5 / Example 1 / src / flux / AppActionTypes.js

    const ActionTypes = {
        INC_COUNTER: 'INC_COUNTER',
        DEC_COUNTER: 'DEC_COUNTER'
    };

    export default ActionTypes;
    ```

- Store:

    ```
    // Chapter 5 / Example 1 / src / flux / AppStore.js

    import { combineReducers, createStore } from 'redux';
    import counterReducer from '../reducers/counterReducer';

    const rootReducer = combineReducers({
        count: counterReducer            // reducer created later on
    });

    const store = createStore(rootReducer);

    export default store;
    ```

Pay attention to two new words—Reducer and rootReducer. rootReducer combines all other reducers into one. Reducer is responsible for generating new versions of the state based on the action that has happened. Reducers can also return the old version of state if the current action is not relevant to the particular Reducer.

- CounterReducer:

```
// Chapter 5 / Example 1 / src / reducers / counterReducer.js

import types from '../flux/AppActionTypes';

const counterReducer = (state = 0, action) => {
    switch (action.type) {
    case types.INC_COUNTER:
        return state + 1;
    case types.DEC_COUNTER:
        return state - 1;
    default:
        return state;
    }
};

export default counterReducer;
```

- Dispatcher:

```
// Chapter 5 / Example 1 / src / flux / AppDispatcher.js
import store from './AppStore';

export default store.dispatch;
```

Great, we have all the Flux pieces, so we can now move on to the actual implementation.

Let's start with simple things first, the view. It should display two Button and one Text components. On a button press, the counter should be increased or decreased, as shown here:

```
// Chapter 5 / Example 1 / src / views / CounterView.js

const CounterView = ({ inc, dec, count }) => (
    <View style={styles.panel}>
        <Button title="-" onPress={dec} />
        <Text>{count}</Text>
        <Button title="+" onPress={inc} />
    </View>
);
```

```
const styles = StyleSheet.create({
    panel: {
        // Check chapter 3: "Style patterns" to learn more on styling
        flex: 1,
        marginTop: 40,
        flexDirection: 'row'
    },
});

export default CounterView;
```

It's time to provide the necessary dependencies to the view: the `inc`, `dec`, and `counter` props. The first two are rather straightforward:

```
// Chapter 5 / Example 1 / src / Counter.js
const increaseAction = () => dispatch({ type: types.INC_COUNTER });
const decreaseAction = () => dispatch({ type: types.DEC_COUNTER });
```

Now we pass them to the view. Here, a number of specific Redux API components will be used. `Provider` is used to provide `store` to connect calls. This is optional—if you really want to do this manually, you can pass `store` directly to `connect`. I highly recommend using `Provider`. `Connect` to create a facade around the dispatch and state. In case of state changes, the component will be automatically re-rendered.

 Facade is another pattern entirely. It is a structural design pattern created to interact with complex APIs. If the typical user is not interested in all of the capabilities, it is handy to provide a function with some defaults already preset on behalf of the user. Such a function is called a `facade` function and is also exposed in the API. The end user can use it a lot quicker, with none of the additional deep-diving that is required for complex and optimized projects.

Check how to use `Provider` and `Connect` in the following snippet:

```
// Chapter 5 / Example 1 / src / Counter.js
...
import { Provider, connect } from 'react-redux';
...

const mapStateToProps = state => ({
    count: state.count,
    inc: increaseAction,
    dec: decreaseAction
});

const CounterContainer = connect(mapStateToProps)(CounterView);
```

```
const CounterApp = () => (
    <Provider store={store}><CounterContainer /></Provider>
);

export default CounterApp;
```

That's it. We have completed the first Redux application.

How Redux fits into Flux

The steps we performed to create a `Counter` app involved connecting Flux pieces. Let's look at the diagram we used:

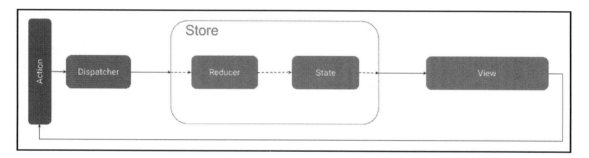

First of all, we have **Actions** that are dispatched. Then the root `Reducer` function is run and each reducer determines whether the state needs to be changed or not. The root **Reducer** returns a new version of **State** and the state is passed to the **View** root. The `connect` function determines whether a particular view should be re-rendered.

 Please note that the previous diagram follows the Flux architecture. The actual Redux implementation, as you could spot in the Counter example, is a little different. The dispatcher is encapsulated by the Store API and exposed as a `store` function.

Moving to Redux

Redux can do more than just very simple state management. It is also known to be performant and beneficial in applications with huge state objects and a lot of business models in it. That said, let's refactor our tasks application to Redux.

The `Tasks` application was developed in the previous chapters. If you have jumped straight to this chapter, please have a look at the application located at `src / Chapter 4 / Example 1_ Todo app with Flux`, in the GitHub repository.

The refactor steps will be similar. Replace existing Flux pieces with Redux ones:

- `ActionTypes`: The actual implementation is okay:

```
const ActionTypes = {
    ADD_TASK: 'ADD_TASK'
};

export default ActionTypes;
```

- `TaskStore.js`: Rename to `AppStore.js`. Now, `store` has just one instance. Additionally, we will need to move the `reduce` function to a separate reducer file. What's left should be converted into a new syntax:

```
// Chapter 5 / Example 2 / src / data / AppStore.js

const rootReducer = combineReducers({ tasks: taskReducer});
const store = createStore(rootReducer);
export default store;
```

- `AppDispatcher.js`: The dispatcher is now part of the store.

```
// Chapter 5 / Example 2 / src / data / AppDispatcher.js
import store from './AppStore';
export default store;
// ATTENTION: To stay consistent with Flux API
// and previous implementation, I return store.
// Store contains dispatch function that is expected.
```

- `taskReducer.js`: This is a new file that we need to create. Its contents, however, are copied from the previous `reduce` function:

```
// Chapter 5 / Example 2 / src / reducers / taskReducer.js
...
import data from '../data/tasks.json';

const taskReducer = (state = Immutable.List([...data.tasks]),
action) => {
    switch (action.type) {
    case TasksActionTypes.ADD_TASK:
        if (!action.task.name) {
            return state;
```

```
        }
        return state.push({
            name: action.task.name,
            description: action.task.description,
            likes: 0
        });
    default:
        return state;
    }
};

export default taskReducer;
```

The last required step is an app container change, as shown here:

```
// Chapter 5 / Example 2 / src / App.js

const mapStateToProps = state => ({ tasks: state.tasks });
const AppContainer = connect(mapStateToProps)(AppView);
const TasksApp = () => (
    <Provider store={store}><AppContainer /></Provider>
);

export default TasksApp;
```

So far, so good. It works. But there are a few things that we skipped here. I will show you what we can do better, but first, let's learn some Redux principles.

Redux as a pattern

Redux, when done right, provides outstanding capabilities, such as **time** travelling and **hot reloading**. Time travelling allows us to see how an application looked over time based on the action log. Hot reloading, on the other hand, allows us to substitute parts of the code without reloading the app.

In this section, we will learn about the core principles of Redux and some commonly recommended approaches.

 Please make the effort to read the Redux documentation. It is a great and free resource to learn how to think in React and Redux. It will also help you expand your use of Redux beyond the React ecosystem, and is available at:
https://redux.js.org/introduction/examples.

Core principles of Redux

Single source of truth: The state of your whole application is stored in an object tree within a single store. Ideally, there should be a single Redux store that can guide your views to render the whole application. This means you should keep all of your states away from class components and place them directly in the Redux store. This will simplify the method with which we will restore the view in tests or when we do a time travel.

Having a single place to store things feels unnatural to some developers, most likely because, over the years on the backend, we have learned that it leads to monolithic architecture. This is not, however, the case in an application environment. An application window is not expected to be scaled vertically to handle a high load of users. Neither should it be used by hundreds of users at the same time on a single device.

State is read-only: The only way to change the state is to emit an action—an object describing what happened. It is vital that we have a single stream that can affect our store. The store is a representation of our application state and should not be mutated by random code. Instead, any code that is interested in changing the state should hand in a **signed paper** that is called an **action object**. This action object represents a known action that is registered in our library, called **action types**. The reducers are the logic that decides the state changes. The immutable state with a single stream of modifying actions is much easier to maintain and supervise. It is quicker to determine whether something has changed or not and when it changed. We can easily create an audit database. Particularly in sensitive industries such as banking, it is a huge advantage.

Changes are made with pure functions: To specify how the state tree is transformed by actions, you write pure reducers. This is a concept that we have not talked about yet. Reducers need to be pure functions. Pure functions guarantee that no external circumstances will affect the result of a function. To put it in a nutshell, reducers cannot perform I/O code, time-constrained code, or code that relies on mutable scoped data.

A pure function is a function that satisfies two requirements:

- It returns the same output, given the same input arguments
- Function execution does not cause any side effects

A good example are common math functions. For instance, an addition function given 1 and 3 always returns 4.

It may not be obvious why all of this is beneficial and should be considered one of the principles. Imagine a situation where a bug was unintentionally introduced into your project in the development phase. Or, even worse, it leaked into production and blew up a critical application during one of the user's sessions. Most likely, you have some error tracking, and you can get the exception and stack trace, which show a long and vague path through minified code. However, you need to fix it, so you try to replay the exact same situation on a local machine of yours and eventually spend three consecutive days just to realize that the problem was some boring race condition. Imagine, instead, that you had a single stream of actions (no random interchanging of untracked conditions) that you track and log. Also, your entire app relies on a state that can only be changed based on the stream of actions. In case of failure, all you need to store in order to reply to the situation is the action trace. Voila, I've just saved you a day or two.

When I learned Redux with similar examples, I still struggled to understand why pure functions are so important here. Playing with time-traveling within the Redux tab for Chrome allowed me to see it more clearly in the flesh. When you go back and forth with actions, some components that are stateful (that is, that rely on an internal state instead of the Redux one) will not be following along. This is a huge issue as it breaks your time travel, leaving some parts in a future state.

Moving to a single source of truth

It's time for an exercise. Our new goal is to refactor the Tasks application so that it has a store that is a single source of truth.

To do so, we need to look for places where we rely on a component state instead of the Redux store. So far we have three views:

- `AppView.js`: This has a fairly simple division into header, footer, and main content.
  This is a presentational component and holds no state. Its props are provided by `AppContainer`, which already uses the Redux store. `AppView` delegates main content to the following two sub-views.
- `TaskList.js`: This is a presentational component responsible for displaying to-do tasks in a simple scrollable list. Its props are forwarded by `AppView` from `AppContainer`.
- `AddTaskForm.js`: This is a container component, based on the `TextInput` component. This piece uses an internal state. If possible, we should refactor this.

If you have ever read about React and Redux, you may find this example pretty similar to what you can find for web pages—however, it is not. If you followed this book for the first chapters, you may have a gut instinct as to why; if not, I highly recommend going back for a while to `Chapter 2 > Building Forms > Uncontrolled Inputs`.

Our goal is to somehow move the state from `AddTaskForm` to the Redux store. This is where problems begin. You may have already spotted that `TextInput` is part of the React-Native API and we have no ability to change it. But `TextInput` is a stateful component. This is the first thing you should realize about Redux when building React Native apps—some parts need to be stateful and you cannot work around it.

Luckily, the stateful part of `TextInput` only manages focus. It is highly unlikely that you would need to store information about that in the Redux store. All the other states belong to our `AddTaskForm` component and we can work around it. Let's do that straight away.

In idiomatic Redux, your state should be normalized similarly to the databases. There are known normalization techniques used in SQL databases that usually are based on ID references between entities. You can adopt this approach in your Redux store by using, for the instance, Normalizr library.

First, we will rebuild the `AddTaskForm` component. It needs to dispatch a new action that will trigger a new reducer and alter a new key in the Redux store (we will develop the latter parts later on):

```
// Chapter 5 / Example 3 / src / views / AddTaskForm.js
class AddTaskForm extends React.Component {
    // ...
    handleSubmit = () => {
        if (this.props.taskForm.name) {
            TaskActions.addTask({
                name: this.props.taskForm.name,
                description: this.props.taskForm.description
            });
            this.nameInput.clear();
            this.descriptionInput.clear();
        }
    };

    render = () => (
        <View style={styles.container}>
            <TextInput
                style={styles.input}
                placeholder="Name"
```

```
                    ref={(input) => { this.nameInput = input; }}
                    onChangeText={
                        name => TaskActions.taskFormChange({
                            name,
                            description: this.props.taskForm.description
                        })
                    }
                    value={this.props.taskForm.name}
                />
                <TextInput
                    style={styles.input}
                    placeholder="Description"
                    ref={(input) => { this.descriptionInput = input; }}
                    onChangeText={
                        desc => TaskActions.taskFormChange({
                            name: this.props.taskForm.name,
                            description: desc
                        })
                    }
                    value={this.props.taskForm.description}
                />
                <Button
                    title="Add task"
                    onPress={() => this.handleSubmit()}
                />
            </View>
        );
    }
```

The hardest part is behind us. It's time to create a brand new taskFormReducer, as follows:

```
// Chapter 5 / Example 3 / src / reducers / taskFormReducer.js

export const INITIAL_ADD_TASK_FORM_STATE = {
    name: '',
    description: ''
};

const taskFormReducer = (
    state = INITIAL_ADD_TASK_FORM_STATE,
    action
) => {
    switch (action.type) {
    case TasksActionTypes.TASK_FORM_CHANGE:
        return action.newFormState;
    default:
        return state;
```

```
    }
};

export default taskFormReducer;
```

Following this, add a new action type to `TasksActionTypes`, as demonstrated in this snippet:

```
// Chapter 5 / Example 3 / src / data / TasksActionTypes.js
const ActionTypes = {
    ADD_TASK: 'ADD_TASK',
    TASK_FORM_CHANGE: 'TASK_FORM_CHANGE'
};
```

Then, add the action itself, as shown here:

```
// Chapter 5 / Example 3 / src / data / TaskActions.js
const Actions = {
    // ...
    taskFormChange(newFormState) {
        AppDispatcher.dispatch({
            type: TasksActionTypes.TASK_FORM_CHANGE,
            newFormState
        });
    }
};
```

Next, register a new reducer in `AppStore`, as follows:

```
// Chapter 5 / Example 3 / src / data / AppStore.js
const rootReducer = combineReducers({
    tasks: taskReducer,
    taskForm: taskFormReducer
});
```

In the end, we need to pass the new state along:

```
// Chapter 5 / Example 3 / src / App.js
const mapStateToProps = state => ({
    tasks: state.tasks,
    taskForm: state.taskForm
});
```

We pass it down the component tree up to `AppView`, as shown here:

```
// Chapter 5 / Example 3 / src / views / AppView.js
const AppView = props => (
        // ...
        <AddTaskForm taskForm={props.taskForm} />
        // ...
);
```

Finally, we have connected all the bits. Enjoy your centralized single source of truth Redux store.

 Alternatively, take a look at the `redux-form` library. As of writing this book, it is an industry standard for building forms in Redux. The library can be found at `https://redux-form.com`.

Creating an alternative with MobX

It would be foolish to rely on Redux with no strong alternative. One of such alternatives is MobX, a state management library that is not so opinionated on mutations. MobX comes with as little boilerplate as possible. This is huge compared to Redux, which, being very explicit, requires a lot of boilerplate.

 Here I must stop to remind you that the React ecosystem leans towards explicitness, that is, building apps without too many hidden mechanisms. You control the flow and you see all of the bits that are required for the app to go the full cycle of Flux. It's n surprise, then, that mainstream developers prefer Redux. An interesting fact is that Facebook Open Source is backing the MobX project.

MobX, being more implicit, can hide away some logic built around Observables and provide neat annotations to quickly enhance your stateful components with MobX flow.

Some developers may find it a much better approach, most likely those coming from an object-oriented background who are used to such things. I find MobX a much easier library to start with and develop a prototype or proof-of-concept application. However, as logic is hidden away from me, I'm afraid that some developers will never have a look under the hood. This may lead to poor performance that cannot easily be fixed later on.

Let's see how it feels in action.

Moving to MobX

In this section, we will refactor the Tasks application to use MobX instead of vanilla Flux.

 The Tasks application was developed in the previous chapters. If you have jumped straight to this chapter, please have a look at the application located at `src / Chapter 4 / Example 1_ Todo app with Flux`, in the GitHub repository.

Before we dive in, install the two packages using the following command:

```
yarn add mobx mobx-react
```

Okay, first, let's clean up unneeded pieces:

- `AppDispatcher.js`: Dispatching is done by MobX using observables behind the scenes.
- `TaskActions.js`: Actions will now live in `TaskStore` and work on its state. In MobX, you will most likely end up with many stores, so this is not a big issue—we keep related things together.
- `TasksActionTypes.js`: There is no need to define this. MobX will take care of it internally.

As you can see, before we begin, we have already removed so much overhead. This is one of the biggest advantages of MobX that fans of the library mention.

It's time to rebuild the store in MobX fashion. This will require some new keywords, so read the following snippet carefully:

```javascript
// Chapter 5 / Example 4 / src / data / TaskStore.js
import { configure, observable, action } from 'mobx';
import data from './tasks.json';

// don't allow state modifications outside actions
configure({ enforceActions: true });

export class TaskStore {
    @observable tasks = [...data.tasks]; // default state

    @action addTask(task) {
        this.tasks.push({
            name: task.name,
            description: task.description,
            likes: 0
        });
```

```
    }
}

const observableTaskStore = new TaskStore();
export default observableTaskStore;
```

As you can see, there are three new keywords that I have imported from the MobX library:

- `configure`: This is used to set up our store in such a way as to enforce mutations only by actions.
- `observable`: This is used to enrich property in such a way it can now be observed. If you have some JavaScript background on streams or Observables, it is literally wrapped by these.
- `action`: This is just like any other action but it's used in a decorator fashion.

Finally, we create an instance of the store and pass it along as a default export.

Now we need to expose our new store to the views. To do this, we will use MobX `Provider`, a similar utility to that found in Redux:

```
// Chapter 5 / Example 4 / src / App.js
// ...
import { Provider as MobXProvider } from 'mobx-react/native';
// ...

const App = () => (
    <MobXProvider store={TaskStore}>
        <AppView />
    </MobXProvider>
);

export default App;
```

The last section of the preceding snippet involves refactoring the descendant views.

The `AppView` component provides tasks down to `TaskList` component. Let's now consume tasks from our newly created store:

```
// Chapter 5 / Example 4 / src / views / AppView.js

import { inject, observer } from 'mobx-react/native';

@inject('store') @observer
class AppView extends React.Component {
  render = () => (
      // ...
```

```
            <AddTaskForm />
            <TaskList tasks={this.props.store.tasks} />
            // ...
    );
    }
```

Let's do something similar with `AddTaskForm`, but instead of using `tasks`, we will use the `addTask` function:

```
// Chapter 5 / Example 4 / src / views / AddTaskForm.js
// ...

@inject('store') @observer
class AddTaskForm extends React.Component {
    // ...
    handleSubmit = () => {
        this.props.store.addTask({
            name: this.state.name,
            description: this.state.description
        });
        // ...
    };
    // ...
}
```

That's it! Our app is fully functional again.

Using PropTypes with annotations

If you followed along, you may feel a little lost, as your linter probably started complaining about insufficient or missing `PropTypes`. Let's fix that.

For `AppView`, we are missing `PropTypes` validation for the `tasks` store. When the class is annotated with `@observer`, it is a little tricky—you need to write `PropTypes` for `wrappedComponent`, as shown here:

```
AppView.wrappedComponent.propTypes = {
    store: PropTypes.shape({
        tasks: PropTypes.arrayOf(PropTypes.shape({
            name: PropTypes.string.isRequired,
            description: PropTypes.string.isRequired,
            likes: PropTypes.number.isRequired
        })).isRequired
    }).isRequired
};
```

For `AddTaskForm`, we are missing the `PropTypes` validation for the `addTask` store action. Let's fix this now:

```
AddTaskForm.wrappedComponent.propTypes = {
    store: PropTypes.shape({
        addTask: PropTypes.func.isRequired
    }).isRequired
};
```

That's it, the linter complaints are gone.

Comparing Redux and MobX

One day I was thinking how to compare those two and the following came to mind.

 This section is highly influenced by Preethi Kasireddy's talk at React Conf 2017. Please spend half an hour and watch it. You can find the talk at `https://www.youtube.com/watch?v=76FRrbY18Bs`.

MobX is like system of roads for cars. You create a road map and let people drive. Some will cause accidents, some will drive carefully. Some roads may be limited to one-way to restrict traffic a little, or even shaped in a certain way to allow easier reasoning about the car flow, as in Manhattan. Redux, on the other hand, is like a train. Only one train can move on a track at a time. If there are a few at the same moment and something is holding up the one in front, every other train waits behind, just like in a subway station. Sometimes trains need to transfer people as far as the other side of a continent, and this is also possible. All of this train flow is governed by one (distributed) agency that plans the movement and puts restrictions on the train flow.

Keeping this example in mind, let's take a more technical look at these libraries:

- Redux uses plain objects, while MobX wraps objects into Observables. You may expect me to mention some magic again—no. The brutal truth is that MobX comes at a cost. It needs to wrap observable data and add some weight to each single object or each member of a collection. It is fairly easy to look up just how much data: use `console.log` to see your observable collection.
- Redux manually tracks updates, whereas MobX automatically tracks updates.
- A Redux state is read-only and can be altered by dispatching an action, while a MobX state can be altered at any time, sometimes only by using actions exposed by your Store API. Also, in MobX, actions are not required. You can change state directly.

- In Redux, a state is typically normalized, or at least this is recommended. In MobX, your state is denormalized and computed values are nested.
- Stateless and stateful components: here it may seem difficult. Preethi Kasireddy, in the lecture linked in the preceding information box, mentioned that MobX can be used with smart components only. To some extent, this is true, but there is no distinction here from Redux. Both support presentational components, as these are completely decoupled from state management libraries!
- The learning curve—this is very subjective criteria. Some will find Redux easier, others will find MobX easier. The popular belief is that MobX is easier to learn. I'm an exception to this.
- Redux requires more boilerplate. Being more explicit, this is quite straightforward, but there are libraries that fix this if you don't care. No references will be provided here, as I recommend educated use.
- Redux is much easier to debug. This comes naturally with single flow and easy replay of messages. This is where Redux shines. MobX is more old-school here, a little harder to predict, and not so obvious, even to experienced users.
- Redux wins when it comes to scalability. MobX may pose some maintainability problems, especially in big projects with a lot of connections and a big domain.
- MobX is concise and shines in small, time-constrained projects. If you go to a hackathon, consider using MobX. In big, long-term projects, you would need a more opinionated approach on top of the freedom that MobX gives.
- MobX follows the Flux architecture and does not alter it as much as Redux does. Redux leans towards one global store (although can be used with many!), while MobX is quite flexible with the amount of stores and its examples usually demonstrate similar thinking to the early ideas of Flux.

While using Redux, you need to learn how to deal with different situations and how to structure things. When it comes to dealing with side effects especially, you will need to learn Redux Thunk and possibly Redux Saga, which will be introduced in the following chapter. In MobX, all of this is magically taken care of behind the scenes, using reactive streams. In this respect, MobX is opinionated, but takes one responsibility away from you.

Using system storage in React Native

Those who come from a Native environment are used to persistent storage, such as databases or files. So far, any time our app has been relaunched, it has lost its state. We can fix that using system storage.

For this purpose, we will use the `AsyncStorage` API that comes with React Native:

> *"On iOS, AsyncStorage is backed by native code that stores small values in a serialized dictionary and larger values in separate files. On Android, AsyncStorage will use either RocksDB or SQLite based on what is available."*
> *- From the React Native official documentation, which can be found at:*
> https://facebook.github.io/react-native/docs/asyncstorage.html.

The `AsyncStorage` API is pretty easy to use. First, let's save the data:

```
import { AsyncStorage } from 'react-native';

try {
    await AsyncStorage.setItem('@MyStore:key', 'value');
} catch (error) {
    // Error saving data
}
```

Next, here's how we retrieve a saved value:

```
try {
    const value = await AsyncStorage.getItem('@MyStore:key');
} catch (error) {
    // Error retrieving data
}
```

However, the documentation advises that we use some abstraction with `AsyncStorage`:

> *"It is recommended that you use an abstraction on top of AsyncStorage instead of AsyncStorage directly for anything more than light usage since it operates globally."*
> *- From the React Native official documentation, which can be found at:*
> https://facebook.github.io/react-native/docs/asyncstorage.html.

So, let's follow the standard library, `redux-persist`. The topic of storage is huge and spans a little beyond this book, so I don't want to dive too deep into this.

Let's install the library with the following command:

```
yarn add redux-persist redux-persist-transform-immutable
```

The first step is to enhance our `AppStore` definition with the new persistence middleware, as shown here:

```
// Chapter 5 / Example 5 / src / data / AppStore.js
// ...
import { persistStore, persistReducer } from 'redux-persist';
import immutableTransform from 'redux-persist-transform-immutable';
```

```
import storage from 'redux-persist/lib/storage';

const persistConfig = {
    transforms: [immutableTransform()],
    key: 'root',
    storage
};

const rootReducer = combineReducers({
    // ...
});
const persistedReducer = persistReducer(persistConfig, rootReducer)
const store = createStore(persistedReducer);
export const persistor = persistStore(store);
export default store;
```

As we are done with the configuration, we need to load the state using `PersistGate`. You can provide a custom component to the loading prop if you have one:

```
// Chapter 5 / Example 5 / src / App.js
import store, { persistor } from './data/AppStore';
// ...
const TasksApp = () => (
    <Provider store={store}>
        <PersistGate loading={null} persistor={persistor}>
            <AppContainer />
        </PersistGate>
    </Provider>
);
```

Voila! Whenever you relaunch the application, the state will be loaded from the persistent store, and you will see all of the tasks from the last application launch.

Effect patterns

When working with external data, you need to deal with external factors, such as the network or disk. These factors influence your code, so it needs to be asynchronous. Also, you should strive to decouple it from your predictable parts, as a network is unpredictable and may fail. We call such things side effects and you have already learned a little about them already.

To understand this, I would like to introduce a big word: effect.

> *"We yield plain JavaScript Objects [...]. We call those Objects Effects. An Effect is simply an object that contains some information to be interpreted by the middleware. You can view Effects like instructions to the middleware to perform some operation (e.g., invoke some asynchronous function, dispatch an action to the store, etc.)."*
> *- From the Redux Saga official documentation, which can be found at:*
> `https://redux-saga.js.org/docs/basics/DeclarativeEffects.html`.

Such effects, if used outside of the immediate scope, cause a so-called **side effect**, hence the name. Most commonly, this means a mutation of an outer scope variable.

The absence of side effects is key to mathematical proofs of the correctness of a program. We will dive into this topic later on in `Chapter 9`, *Elements of Functional Programming Patterns*.

Handling side effects

In `Chapter 4`, *Flux Architecture*, you learned what side effects are and what strategies you can follow to decouple them from Views and Store. When using Redux, you should stick to them. However, there are a few neat libraries that have been developed for Redux to solve the problem. You will learn more on them in the following chapter, which is dedicated just to this issue:

> *"We're mixing two concepts that are very hard for the human mind to reason about: mutation and asynchronicity. I call them Mentos and Coke. Both can be great in separation, but together they create a mess. Libraries like React attempt to solve this problem in the view layer by removing both asynchrony and direct DOM manipulation. However, managing the state of your data is left up to you. This is where Redux enters."*
> *- Official Redux documentation*

Summary

In this chapter, we discussed the importance of stores in our architecture. You learned how to shape your application in order to fulfill different business needs, from very fragile ones using a mixed approach of state and global state, to sophisticated ones allowing time-traveling and UI reconstruction.

Instead of focusing on one mainstream solution, that is, Redux, we also explored the quite different approach of the MobX library. We found it great in many areas, such as rapid prototyping and small projects, and you now know when and in which projects it is wise to choose MobX over Redux.

Further reading

- Redux official documentation:
  `https://redux.js.org/`.
  This is a particularly useful part of the documentation:
  `https://redux.js.org/faq`.
- *Introduction of Redux Time Travel and Hot Reloading* by Dan Abramov, on React Europe:

  `https://www.youtube.com/watch?v=xsSnOQynTHs`.
- Dan Abramov's courses on Egghead:

  `https://egghead.io/instructors/dan-abramov`.
- Redux GitHub page with closed issues. This contains a ton of useful discussions:

  `https://github.com/reduxjs/redux/issues?q=is%3Aissue+is%3Aclosed`.
- Netflix JavaScript Talks: *RxJS + Redux + React = Amazing!*

  `https://www.youtube.com/watch?v=AslncyG8whg`.
- *How Airbnb Is Using React Native*:
  `https://www.youtube.com/watch?v=8qCociUB6aQ`.
  This is not strictly on store patterns but illustrates how to think about big production applications, such as Airbnb.

- You might need Redux:

  `https://www.youtube.com/watch?v=2iPE5l3cl_sfeature=youtu.bet=2h7m28s`.
- Last but not least, a very important topic brought to you by the Redux author:

  You Might Not Need Redux:

  `https://medium.com/@dan_abramov/you-might-not-need-redux-be46360cf367`.

6
Data Transfer Patterns

In this chapter, we will learn how to send and receive data in the React Native application. Firstly, we will make our application more dynamic and dependent on the backend servers. You will learn about the Thunk pattern, which fits into Flux really neatly. Then, we will dive into a more advanced library, redux-saga, which is based on an effect pattern. Both of the solutions will enable our application to seamlessly exchange data with the server. I will also give you a little introduction to more advanced communication patterns, such as `HATEOAS` and `GraphQL`. Although those two patterns are rarely crucial for a React Native developer, you will find it much easier to understand if, one day, those patterns become popular within the React Native world too.

In this chapter, you will learn how to do the following:

- Create a fake API
- Fetch data from the backend and store it in the application
- Design action creators and decouple fetching logic from the containers
- Use Redux Thunk to conditionally dispatch actions
- Write your own iterators and generators
- Benefit from sagas that heavily rely on generators

Preparation

In order to test various APIs without relying on external sources, we will create our own local API. You do not need to know any backend language, nor how to expose an API. In this chapter, we will use a special library that builds an API based on the JSON file that we provide.

So far, we have made a neat application displaying tasks. Now, instead of loading the local data file, let's use our own REST API. Clone the task application to start. (I will be using code from example two in the directory for `Chapter 5`, *Store Patterns*.)

Representational State Transfer (REST) is a set of rules that put constraints on web services. One of the crucial requirements is statelessness, which guarantees the server will not store the client's data, but instead rely only on the request data. This should be sufficient enough to send a reply to the client.

In order to create a fake API, we will use the `json-server` library. The library expects a JSON file; most examples call it `db.json`. Based on the file, the library creates a static API that sends data on requests.

Let's start by installing the library with the following command:

```
yarn global add json-server
```

If you prefer to avoid `global`, please remember to provide a relative path to the `node_modules/json-server/bin` in the following scripts.

The JSON file for the library should look like the following:

```
{
  "tasks": [
    // task objects separated by comma
  ]
}
```

Luckily, our `tasks.json` file fits this requirement. We can now launch our local server. Open `package.json` and add a new script called `server`, as follows:

```
// src / Chapter 6 / Example 1 / package.jsonn
// ...
"scripts": {
  // ...
  "server": "json-server --watch ./src/data/tasks.json"
},
// ...
```

You can now type `yarn run server` to launch it. The data will be exposed at `http://localhost:3000/tasks`. Simply access the URL with your browser to check if it works. A correctly set up server should print data like the following:

```
[
  {
    "name": "Task 1",
    "description": "Task 1 description",
```

```
    "likes": 239
  },
  // ... other task objects
]
```

We can now proceed further to learn how to work with endpoints.

Fetching data with the built-in function

To begin, let's start with something fairly basic. React Native implements the Fetch API, which is nowadays a standard for making REST API calls.

Refactoring to activity indicator

Currently, we have a default task list being loaded from the file in `taskReducer.js`. To be honest, loading from either the file or API can be time consuming. It will be better initially to set the task list to empty the array and provide feedback to the user with a spinner or text message, informing them that the data is being loaded. We will implement this along with the change to the Fetch API.

First, remove data import from the file in the reducer. Change the declaration from the following:

```
(state = Immutable.List([...data.tasks]), action) => {
    // ...
}
```

And replace it with the code in this snippet:

```
(state = Immutable.List([]), action) => {
    // ...
}
```

 Loading data from a file is also a side effect and should undergo similarly restrictive patterns to data fetching. Don't be fooled by the previous implementation that we used to synchronously load data. This shortcut was taken only to concentrate on the specific learning material.

Launch the application to see an empty list. Let's now add a loading indicator, as follows:

```
import { View, Text, StyleSheet, ActivityIndicator } from 'react-native';
// ...
const TaskList = ({ tasks, isLoading }) => (
    <View>
        {isLoading
            ? <ActivityIndicator size="large" color="#0000ff" />
            : tasks.map((task, index) => (
                // ...
            ))
        }
    </View>
);
```

In some cases, where the loading is taking a long time, you will need to handle a more complex scenario: the data is loading, but the user may still add tasks in the meantime. In the previous implementation, the task would not be shown until the data is retrieved from the server. The easy fix for this is to always show tasks if we have any, regardless of the isLoading prop, which would mean that some other data is expected:

```
// src / Chapter 6 / Example 2 / src / views / TaskList.js
const TaskList = ({ tasks, isLoading }) => (
    <View>
        {isLoading && <ActivityIndicator size="large" color="#0000ff" />}
        {tasks.map((task, index) => (
            // ...
        ))}
    </View>
);
```

As we have a loading indicator that is shown based on the isLoading prop, we need to think about other states that our fetching process may produce.

Handling error scenarios

Fetch, in most use cases, will require three states:

- **START**: A fetch start, which should cause isLoading to be true
- **SUCCESS**: Data was fetched successfully
- **ERROR**: Fetch could not retrieve data; an appropriate error message should be shown

The last state we need to handle is error. There are a few approaches to this with respect to user experience guidelines:

- Displaying an error message within the list—this provides a clear message for those who care about the data in the table. It may include a clickable link or a button to retry. You may mix this approach with the ones that follow.
- Displaying a floating notification about the failure—this shows the message about the error in one of the corners. The message may disappear after a few seconds.
- Displaying an error modal—this stops the user to notify them about the error; it may contain actions such as retry, and dismiss.

The approach I would like to take here is the first one. It is fairly easy to implement—we need to add an `error` prop and, based on it, display a message:

```
const TaskList = ({
    tasks, isLoading, hasError, errorMsg
}) => (
    <View>
        {hasError &&
            <View><Text>{errorMsg}</Text></View>}
        {hasError && isLoading &&
            <View><Text>Fetching again...</Text></View>}
        {isLoading && <ActivityIndicator size="large" color="#0000ff" />}
        {tasks.map((task, index) => (
            // ...
        ))}
    </View>
);
// ...
TaskList.defaultProps = {
    errorMsg: 'Error has occurred while fetching tasks.'
};
```

Naive stateful component fetching

Now, let's fetch some data and make our markup fully usable. First, we will follow the approach for beginners in React: using `fetch` in one of the stateful components. In our case, it will be `App.js`:

```
// src / Chapter 6 / Example 2 / src / App.js
class TasksFetchWrapper extends React.Component {
    constructor(props) {
        super(props);
```

```
        // Default state of the component
        this.state = {
            isLoading: true,
            hasError: false,
            errorMsg: '',
            tasks: props.tasks
        };
    }

    componentDidMount() {
        // Start fetch and on completion set state to either data or
        // error
        return fetch('http://localhost2:3000/tasks')
            .then(response => response.json())
            .then((responseJSON) => {
                this.setState({
                    isLoading: false,
                    tasks: Immutable.List(responseJSON)
                });
            })
            .catch((error) => {
                this.setState({
                    isLoading: false,
                    hasError: true,
                    errorMsg: error.message
                });
            });
    }

    render = () => (
        <AppView
            tasks={this.state.tasks}
            isLoading={this.state.isLoading}
            hasError={this.state.hasError}
            errorMsg={this.state.errorMsg}
        />
    );
}

// State from redux passed to wrapper.
const mapStateToProps = state => ({ tasks: state.tasks });
const AppContainer = connect(mapStateToProps)(TasksFetchWrapper);
```

This approach has a number of disadvantages. First, it does not follow the Fetch API documentation. Let's read this crucial quote:

> *"The Promise returned from fetch won't reject on HTTP error status even if the response is an HTTP 404 or 500. Instead, it will resolve normally (with ok status set to false), and it will only reject on network failure or if anything prevented the request from completing."*
> *- Fetch API documentation, available at:*
> `https://developer.mozilla.org/en-US/docs/Web/API/Fetch_API/Using_Fetch.`

As you can see, the preceding implementation lacks HTTP error handling.

The second issue is state duplication, where we maintain a Redux state, but then copy tasks to the local component state, and even override it with what has been fetched. We could be more concerned about what we have in the tasks already by concatenating both arrays, and find a way to avoid storing the tasks again.

Also, if the Redux state changes, then the previous component will entirely neglect the update. This is too bad—let's find a way to fix this.

The Thunk pattern and Redux Thunk

In this section, we will learn about the **Thunk pattern** and how to use it with the **Redux Thunk** library. To begin, we will need to refactor our naive and faulty implementation from the previous section to one using Redux.

Lifting the state to Redux

Instead of relying on the component state, let's lift it to a Redux store. Pay attention to the `Immutable.Map` we use here. Also, the `ADD_TASK` action is now using the `update` function from `Immutable.js`:

```
// src / Chapter 6 / Example 3 / src / reducers / taskReducer.js

const taskReducer = (state = Immutable.Map({
    entities: Immutable.List([]),
    isLoading: false,
    hasError: false,
    errorMsg: ''
}), action) => {
    switch (action.type) {
```

```
        case TasksActionTypes.ADD_TASK:
            if (!action.task.name) {
                return state;
            }
            return state.update('entities', entities => entities.push({
                name: action.task.name,
                description: action.task.description,
                likes: 0
            }));
        default:
            return state;
    }
};
```

As we have changed the reducer, we need to fix the stateful component. Instead of having its own state, it should delegate to the Redux store through actions. However, we will implement these actions later on:

```
// src / Chapter 6 / Example 3 / src / App.js
class TasksFetchWrapper extends React.Component {
    componentDidMount() {
        TaskActions.fetchStart();
        return fetch('http://localhost:3000/tasks')
            .then(response => response.json())
            .then((responseJSON) => {
                TaskActions.fetchComplete(Immutable.List(responseJSON));
            })
            .catch((error) => TaskActions.fetchError(error));
    }

    render = () => <AppView tasks={this.props.tasks} />;
}
```

 It is wise to move fetching logic to a separate service. This will enable other components to share the same function once they need to trigger fetch too. This is your homework.

Instead of `componentDidMount`, you could dispatch actions to a constructor. This, however, could create the temptation to refactor to the function component. This would be a disaster, as you would start fetching on every re-render. Also, `componentDidMount` is safer for us, as in case of any computations that could slow down the application in context of the actions, we are 100% sure that the user can already see `ActivityIndicator`.

Now, move to the actions implementation. You should be able to write them on your own. In case of any trouble, see `src / Chapter 6 / Example 3 / src / data / TaskActions.js`. We will now focus on extending the reducer. This is quite some work, as we need to handle all three action types: FETCH_START, FETCH_COMPLETE, and FETCH_ERROR, as shown here:

```
// src / Chapter 6 / Example 3 / src / reducers / taskReducer.js
const taskReducer = (state = Immutable.Map({
    // ...
}), action) => {
    switch (action.type) {
    case TasksActionTypes.ADD_TASK: {
        // ...
    }
    case TasksActionTypes.TASK_FETCH_START: {
        return state.update('isLoading', () => true);
    }
    case TasksActionTypes.TASK_FETCH_COMPLETE: {
        const noLoading = state.update('isLoading', () => false);
        return noLoading.update('entities', entities => (
            // For every task we update the state
            // Homework: do this in bulk
            action.tasks.reduce((acc, task) => acc.push({
                name: task.name,
                description: task.description,
                likes: 0
            }), entities)
        ));
    }
    case TasksActionTypes.TASK_FETCH_ERROR: {
        const noLoading = state.update('isLoading', () => false);
        const errorState = noLoading.update('hasError', () => true);
        return errorState.update('errorMsg', () => action.error.message);
    }
    default: {
        return state;
    }
    }
};
```

This is basically it. In the end, you will also need to update views to use a new structure, `Immutable.Map`, as follows:

```
// src / Chapter 6 / Example 3 / src / views / AppView.js
// ...
<TaskList
    tasks={props.tasks.get('entities')}
    isLoading={props.tasks.get('isLoading')}
    hasError={props.tasks.get('hasError')}
    errorMsg={props.tasks.get('errorMsg')}
/>
// ...
```

There are a few improvements to be made to this code. I will not touch on them right now, as those are advanced topics and involve more general JavaScript functional programming concepts. You will learn about lenses and selectors in `Chapter 8`, *JavaScript and ECMAScript Patterns*.

Benefits of refactoring to Redux

It may be tricky to see the benefits of the previous refactor. Some of these refactors shine only days after you make them. Take, for example, the need to re-fetch the tasks on a given event. This event happens in a completely different part of the app and is not connected to the task list. In the naive implementation, you would need to deal with the update process and keep everything up to date. You would also need to expose a `fetch` function to another component. This would tightly couple those two. Disaster. Instead, as you can see, you would likely prefer to duplicate fetching logic to the second separated component. Again, you would end up with code duplication. Therefore, you would create a parent service shared by those two components. Unfortunately, the fetching is tightly coupled with the state, hence you would move state to the service as well. Then, you would make some hacks, such as using closure to store the data within the service. As you can see, this is a smooth solution to these problems.

When using the Redux store, however, you have one centralized state that is updated only through reducers. Fetching is sending data to the reducers using carefully designed actions. Fetch can be performed in a separated service that is shared by the components that need to fetch tasks. We will now introduce a library that makes all of these things cleaner.

Using Redux Thunk

In classic Redux, with no middleware, you cannot dispatch something that is not a pure object. With Redux Thunk, you can delay the dispatch by dispatching a function:

> *"Redux Thunk middleware allows you to write action creators that return a function instead of an action. The thunk can be used to delay the dispatch of an action, or to dispatch only if a certain condition is met. The inner function receives the store methods dispatch and getState as parameters."*
> *- Redux Thunk official documentation, available at:*
> `https://github.com/reduxjs/redux-thunk`.

For instance, you can dispatch a function. Such a function has two arguments: `dispatch` and `getState`. This function does not reach the Redux reducers yet. It only delays the old-fashioned Redux dispatch until necessary checks are performed, for instance, checks based on current state. Once we are ready to dispatch, we use the `dispatch` function provided as a `function` argument:

```
function incrementIfOdd() {
  return (dispatch, getState) => {
    const { counter } = getState();

    if (counter % 2 === 0) {
      return;
    }

    dispatch(increment());
  };
}

dispatch(incrementIfOdd())
```

In the previous section, I pointed out that the `fetch` call could be a separate function. If you haven't done the homework, here is an example refactor:

```
const fetchTasks = () => {
    TaskActions.fetchStart();
    return fetch('http://localhost:3000/tasks')
        .then(response => response.json())
        .then((responseJSON) => {
            TaskActions.fetchComplete(Immutable.List(responseJSON));
        })
        .catch(error => TaskActions.fetchError(error));
};

class TasksFetchWrapper extends React.Component {
```

```
        componentDidMount = () => this.props.fetchTasks();
        render = () => <AppView tasks={this.props.tasks} />;
    }

    const mapStateToProps = state => ({ tasks: state.tasks });
    const mapDispatchToProps = dispatch => ({ fetchTasks });
    const AppContainer = connect(mapStateToProps,
    mapDispatchToProps)(TasksFetchWrapper);
```

However, our so-called `ActionCreators` are tightly coupled to `dispatch`, and therefore not only create actions, but also `dispatch`. Let's loosen their responsibilities by removing dispatching:

```
// Before
const Actions = {
addTask(task) {
        AppDispatcher.dispatch({
type: TasksActionTypes.ADD_TASK,
            task
        });
    },
    fetchStart() {
        AppDispatcher.dispatch({
type: TasksActionTypes.TASK_FETCH_START
        });
    },
    // ...
};

// After
const ActionCreators = {
    addTask: task => ({
type: TasksActionTypes.ADD_TASK,
        task
    }),
    fetchStart: () => ({
type: TasksActionTypes.TASK_FETCH_START
    }),
    // ...
};
```

Now, we need to make sure to dispatch the preceding actions to the relevant places. This can be achieved by passing to `dispatch`, as follows:

```
const ActionTriggers = {
    addTask: dispatch => task => dispatch(ActionCreators.addTask(task)),
    fetchStart: dispatch => () => dispatch(ActionCreators.fetchStart()),
    fetchComplete: dispatch =>
```

```
        tasks => dispatch(ActionCreators.fetchComplete(tasks)),
    fetchError: dispatch =>
        error => dispatch(ActionCreators.fetchError(error))
};
```

 For those experienced in programming, this step may look a little like we are repeating ourselves. We are duplicating function parameters and the only thing we gain is the invocation of dispatch. We can fix this with functional patterns. Such improvements will be made as part of Chapter 8, *JavaScript and ECMAScript Patterns*.

Additionally, please note that in this book, I'm not writing many tests. Once you make writing tests a habit, you will quickly appreciate such easily testable code.

Having done this, we can now adjust our container component, as shown:

```
// src / Chapter 6 / Example 4 / src / App.js
export const fetchTasks = (dispatch) => {
    TaskActions.fetchStart(dispatch)();
    return fetch('http://localhost:3000/tasks')
        .then(response => response.json())
        .then(responseJSON =>
TaskActions.fetchComplete(dispatch)(Immutable.List(responseJSON)))
        .catch(TaskActions.fetchError(dispatch));
};
// ...
const mapDispatchToProps = dispatch => ({
fetchTasks: () => fetchTasks(dispatch),
    addTask: TaskActions.addTask(dispatch)
});
```

Okay, this is a great refactor, but where is Redux Thunk? This is a very good question. I did prolong this example on purpose. In many React and React Native projects, I see overuse of Redux Thunk and other libraries. I don't want you to be another developer who does not understand the purpose of Redux Thunk and abuses the power that it gives.

Redux Thunk primarily lets you decide to dispatch conditionally. The access to dispatch through the Thunk function is not something extraordinary. The main benefit is the second argument, getState. This lets you access the current state and decide based on the values there.

Such powerful tools may lead you to create impure reducers. How? Instead of creating a real reducer, you would create a **setter reducer**, working similarly to the set function in classes. Such a reducer would be invoked only to set the value; however, the value would be computed in the Thunk function, using the `getState` function. This is completely anti-pattern and may lead to a serious breaking of race conditions.

Now that we know the dangers, let's move on to the real usages of Thunks. Imagine a situation where you would like to make a decision conditionally. How would you access the state to make an `if` statement? This gets complicated once we use the `connect()` function in Redux. The `mapDispatchToProps` function that we pass to `connect` does not have access to the state. But we need it, so here comes a valid usage of Redux Thunk.

The following is good to know: how would we make an escape hatch if we could not use Redux Thunk? We could pass part of the state to the `render` function, and then invoke the original function with the expected state. The `if` statement could be done with a regular `if` in JSX. This could, however, lead to serious performance issues.

It's time to use Redux Thunk in our case. You may have noticed that our dataset does not contain IDs. This is a huge problem if we fetch tasks two times, as we have no mechanism to tell which tasks have been added and which are already present in our UI. The current approach of adding all of the fetched tasks would lead to task duplication. The first prevention mechanism for our broken architecture is to stop the fetch if `isLoading` is `true`.

A real-life scenario would either use IDs or refresh all the tasks on fetch. If so, `ADD_TASK` would need to guarantee changes in the backend server. In the era of Progressive Web Apps, we need to stress this problem even further. Take the case where a connection is lost before adding a new task. If your UI adds the task locally and schedules a backend update, once the network connection is resolved you may run into a race condition: this means that tasks are being refreshed before your `ADD_TASK` update is propagated in the backend system. As a result, you would end up with a task list that will not contain the added task until you refetch all tasks from the backend. This may be extremely misleading and should not happen in any financial institution.

Let's implement this naive prevention mechanism to illustrate the capabilities of Redux Thunk. First, install the library with the following command:

```
yarn add redux-thunk
```

Then, we need to apply `thunk` middleware to Redux, as shown here:

```
// src / Chapter 6 / Example 4 / src / data / AppStore.js
import { combineReducers, createStore, applyMiddleware } from 'redux';
import thunk from 'redux-thunk';
// ...
const store = createStore(rootReducer, applyMiddleware(thunk));
```

From now on, we can dispatch functions. Let's now fix our `fetch` function to avoid multiple requests:

```
// src / Chapter 6 / Example 5 / src / App.js
export const fetchTasks = (dispatch, getState) => {
    if (!getState().tasks.isLoading) {
        // ...
    }
    return null;
};
// ...
const mapDispatchToProps = dispatch => ({
    fetchTasks: () => dispatch(fetchTasks),
    // ...
});
```

As you can see, this is quite a simple use case. Please use Redux Thunk wisely and do not abuse the power that it gives you.

Understanding the Thunk pattern

Thunk is another pattern that isn't specific to React or Redux. Actually, it is used quite widely in many hardcore solutions, such as compilers.

Thunk is a pattern that delays evaluation until it cannot be avoided. One of the beginner examples that explains this is simple addition. An example is shown here:

```
// immediate calculation, x equals 3
let x = 1 + 2;

// delayed calculation until function call, x is a thunk
let x = () => 1 + 2;
```

Some more complex usages, for instance, in functional languages, may rely on this pattern throughout the entire language. Hence, computations are performed only when the end application layer needs them. Usually, no ahead-of-time computations are performed, as such optimizations are the responsibility of the developer.

The saga pattern and Redux Saga

So far, we can perform simple API calls using `fetch`, and we know how to organize our code to be reusable. In some areas, however, we could do better if our application required it. Before we dive in Redux Saga, I want to introduce two new patterns: iterator and generator.

> *"Processing each of the items in a collection is a very common operation. JavaScript provides a number of ways of iterating over a collection, from simple for loops to map and filter. Iterators and Generators bring the concept of iteration directly into the core language and provide a mechanism for customizing the behavior of for...of loops."*
> *- JavaScript guide on MDN web docs at:*
> `https://developer.mozilla.org/en-US/docs/Web/JavaScript/Guide/`
> `Iterators_and_Generators.`

Introduction to the iterator pattern

The iterator, as the name suggests, lets you iterate over a collection. To be able to do so, the collection needs to implement an iterable interface. In JavaScript, there are no interfaces, hence the iterator simply implements a single function.

> *"An object is an iterator when it knows how to access items from a collection one at a time, while keeping track of its current position within that sequence. In JavaScript an iterator is an object that provides a next method which returns the next item in the sequence. This method returns an object with two properties: done and value."*
> *- JavaScript guide on MDN web docs*
> `https://developer.mozilla.org/en-US/docs/Web/JavaScript/Guide/`
> `Iterators_and_Generators`

The following is an example of such a function from MDN web docs:

```
function createArrayIterator(array) {
    var nextIndex = 0;

    return {
        next: function() {
```

```
            return nextIndex < array.length ?
                {value: array[nextIndex++], done: false} :
                {done: true};
        }
    };
}
```

The generator pattern

Generators are similar to iterators; here, however, you iterate over carefully designed breakpoints within a function. A generator returns an iterator. The returned iterator iterates over the mentioned breakpoints and, each time, returns some value from the function.

To signal that the function is a generator, we use a special * sign, for instance, `function*` `idGenerator()`. Please find an example generator function in the following snippet. Generators use the `yield` keyword to return the current iteration step value. The iterator will resume in the next line if its `next()` function is invoked, as seen here:

```
function* numberGenerator(numMax) {
    for (let i = 0; i < numMax; i += 1) {
        yield console.log(i);
    }
}
const threeNumsIterator = numberGenerator(3);

// logs 0
threeNumsIterator.next();
// logs 1
threeNumsIterator.next();
// logs 2
threeNumsIterator.next();
// logs nothing, the returned object contains a key 'done' set to true
threeNumsIterator.next();
```

First, we create a `generator` function. The `Generator` function expects one argument. Based on the argument provided, the generator knows when to stop generating new numbers. After the function, we create an example number iterator and iterate over its values.

Redux Saga

Redux Saga rely heavily on the generator pattern. Thanks to this approach, we can decouple side effects entirely into sagas that act as if they were a separate thread. It is convenient and provides a few advantages to Thunk functions in the long run. Some of those rely on composability, with sagas being easy to test and giving cleaner flows to execute asynchronous code. All of these may sound unclear right now, so let's dive in to get a better understanding.

This book does not touch much on React, Redux, and React Native testing. This topic would lengthen this book significantly and, I believe, deserves a separate book. However, I will stress how important it is to test your code. This information box is to remind you about testing in Redux Sagas. In different places on the internet (GitHub, forums, Stack Overflow) I have seen this mentioned over and over again: sagas are much easier to test than Thunks. Check this on your own—you will not regret it.

First, do the beginner steps of installing the library and applying the middleware. These steps can be found in the official Redux Saga README file, available at `https://redux-saga.js.org/`.

It's time to create the first saga and add it to our `rootSaga`. Do you remember the case with fetching tasks? They could be requested from many places (many decoupled widgets or features). The approach of saga is similar to our previous solutions, so let's see how it can be implemented in the following example:

```
// src / Chapter 6 / Example 6 / src / sagas / fetchTasks.js
function* fetchTasks() {
    const tasks = yield call(ApiFetch, 'tasks');
    if (tasks.error) {
        yield put(ActionCreators.fetchError(tasks.error));
    } else {
        const json = yield call([tasks.response, 'json']);
        yield put(ActionCreators.fetchComplete(Immutable.List(json)));
    }
}

// whereas ApiFetch is our own util function
// you will want to make a separate file for it
// and take care of environmental variables to determine right endpoint
const ApiFetch = path => fetch(`http://localhost:3000/${path}`)
    .then(response => ({ response }))
    .catch(error => ({ error }));
```

Our `fetchTasks` saga is really simple: first, it fetches tasks, then checks if an error happened, and either dispatches an error event or a successful event with the fetched data attached.

How do we trigger the `fetchTasks` saga? To convince you why sagas are powerful, let's even push it further. Let's say our code base is decoupled and a few features will request tasks at almost the same time. How do we prevent multiple fetch task jobs being triggered? Redux Saga library has a ready-made solution for this: the `throttle` function.

> *"throttle(ms, pattern, saga, ...args) Spawns a saga on an action dispatched to the Store that matches pattern. After spawning a task it's still accepting incoming actions into the underlaying buffer, keeping at most 1 (the most recent one), but in the same time holding up with spawning new task for ms milliseconds (hence its name - throttle). Purpose of this is to ignore incoming actions for a given period of time while processing a task."*
> *- Official Redux Saga documentation:*
> `https://redux-saga.js.org/docs/api/.`

Our use case will be very straightforward:

```
// src / Chapter 6 / Example 6 / src / sagas / fetchTasks.js
function* watchLastFetchTasks() {
    yield throttle(2000, TasksActionTypes.TASK_FETCH_START, fetchTasks);
}
```

The `fetchTasks` function will be executed on the `TASK_FETCH_START` event. For two seconds, the same event will not cause another `fetchTasks` function execution.

That's it. One of the last few things is to add the preceding saga to `rootSaga`. This is not a very interesting part but, if you are curious, I recommend you check the full example in the code repository, available at `https://github.com/Ajdija/hands-on-design-patterns-with-react-native.`

Redux Saga benefits

In more complex applications with well defined routines, Redux Saga outshines Redux Thunk. Once you run into a need to cancel, rerun, or reply to part of the flow, it is not immediately obvious how these can be done using Thunks or plain Redux. With composable sagas and well-maintained iterators, you can do it with ease. Even the official documentation provides recipes for such problems. (See the *Further reading* section at the end of this chapter for reference.)

The dark side of such a powerful library is its problematic usage in brownfield applications. Such applications, with features possibly written in a promise-based or Thunk fashion, may require a significant refactor in order to be used with sagas with the ease found in greenfield apps. For instance, it is not so easy to call a saga from the Thunk function, nor you can wait on the dispatched function as you would on the promise within sagas. There are probably good hacks to connect both worlds, but is it really worth it?

Summary

In this chapter, we focused heavily on networking patterns and the side effects that come along with them. We went through simple patterns and then used the available tools on the market. You have learned about the Thunk pattern, along with iterator and generator patterns. All three of these patterns will be useful in your future programming career, whether it is in React Native or not.

As for the React ecosystem, you have learned the basics of the Redux Thunk and Redux Saga libraries. Both of them solve some of the challenges that come with large scale applications. Use them wisely and bear in mind all of the warnings I have placed within this chapter.

Now that we know how to display data, style it, and fetch it, we are ready to learn some application building patterns. Namely, in the next chapter, you will learn navigational patterns. In React Native, there are plenty of solutions to these problems and I'm more than happy to teach you how to choose the one that matches your project's needs.

Further reading

- Writing Tests—Redux Official Documentation:
  `https://redux.js.org/recipes/writing-tests`.
- Implementing Undo History—Redux Official Documentation:
  `https://redux.js.org/recipes/implementing-undo-history`.
- Server rendering—Redux Official Documentation:
  `https://redux.js.org/recipes/server-rendering`.

- Normalizing state—Redux Official Documentation:
  `https://redux.js.org/recipes/structuring-reducers/normalizing-state-shape`.
  This is important in the context of networking patterns. Some of your data that is fetched from backend systems will need to be normalized.
- Async actions—Redux Official Documentation:
  `https://redux.js.org/advanced/async-actions`.
- Redux Saga recipes—Redux Saga Official Documentation:
  `https://redux-saga.js.org/docs/recipes/`.
  This resource is particularly valuable for its recipes for throttling, debouncing, and undo using sagas.
- Redux Saga channels – Redux Saga Official Documentation:

  > *"Until now we've used the take and put effects to communicate with the Redux Store. Channels generalize those Effects to communicate with external event sources or between Sagas themselves. They can also be used to queue specific actions from the Store."*
  > *- Redux Saga Official Documentation:*
  > `https://redux-saga.js.org/docs/advanced/Channels.html`.

- Idiomatic redux thoughts on Thunks, sagas, abstraction, and reusability:
  `https://blog.isquaredsoftware.com/2017/01/idiomatic-redux-thoughts-on-thunks-sagas-abstraction-and-reusability/`.
- Resources library: React Redux Links/Redux Side effects:
  `https://github.com/markerikson/react-redux-links/blob/master/redux-side-effects.md`.
- A Saga on Sagas:

  > *"The term saga is commonly used in discussions of CQRS to refer to a piece of code that coordinates and routes messages between bounded contexts and aggregates. However, [...] we prefer to use the term process manager to refer to this type of code artifact."*
  > *A Saga on Sagas - Microsoft Docs:*
  > `https://docs.microsoft.com/en-us/previous-versions/msp-n-p/jj591569(v=pandp.10)`.

- GraphQL—another approach to side effects. GraphQL is a query language for your API, both on the frontend and backend side. Find out more here:
  `https://graphql.org/learn/`.

- Redux Observable—a Thunk and sagas competitor. Introduces Reactive Programming patterns:
  `https://github.com/redux-observable/redux-observable`.
  Please also check out RxJS, a reactive programming library for JavaScript:
  `https://github.com/reactivex/rxjs`.
- Representational State Transfer :
  `https://en.wikipedia.org/wiki/Representational_state_transfer`.
- HATEOAS (a component of the REST architecture):
  `https://en.wikipedia.org/wiki/HATEOAS`.

7
Navigation Patterns

The crucial part of almost every application is navigation. To this day, this topic gives headaches to many React Native developers. Let's see which libraries are available and which one will suit your project. This chapter starts with a breakdown of the available libraries. Then, we will introduce a new project and play with it. We will focus on one library at a time. Once we finish this, I will walk you through the patterns that are used, and what these imply, while you write the navigation code. Remember to try the code on your machine and your phone.

In this chapter, you will learn about the following:

- Why are there many alternative libraries for routing in React Native?
- What are the challenges that navigation libraries face?
- What is the difference between native navigation and JavaScript navigation?
- How to use Tab navigation, Drawer navigation, and Stack navigation.
- The basics of native solutions: you will eject the Create React Native App for the first time.

React Native navigation alternatives

Usually, if you are a beginner and you try to Google for *React Native navigation*, you will end up with a headache. The number of available alternatives is high. There are a few reasons why this is so:

- Some early libraries are not maintained anymore, as maintainers have simply quit
- Some companies with resources started a library and then changed their employees focus to other things
- Some solutions are proven to be inefficient, or a better solution is implemented
- There is an architectural reason for different approaches, which leads to a need to maintain different solutions

We will focus on the last point here, as it is vital to understand which library fits your needs. We will discuss the solutions so that, at the end of this chapter, you will know which library to choose for your project.

Designers navigation patterns

Before we dive into the world of libraries, I would like to show you different ways of designing navigation in your application. Usually, this is work for the project's designer; however, once you understand the trade-offs, it will be easier to add a code pattern layer on top of it.

The mobile app consists of screens and transitions. Altogether, these can be represented by the following diagram:

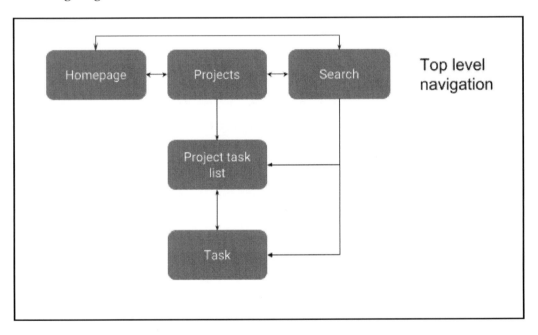

This is an example diagram representing the screens of a tasks application

The main takeaways from the preceding diagram are as follows:

- Each app consists of top-level screens (**Homepage**, **Projects**, and **Search**)
- From top-level screens, you can navigate forward and deeper down the tree (**Projects** => **Project task list**)
- Sometimes, you transition backwards (**Task** => **Project task list**)

With this in mind, let's look into the components that will help us make these transitions.

Navigation to top-level screens

Navigation to top-level screens is usually done using one or more of the following three alternatives:

- Classical bottom navigation, like the one we already implemented. This usually uses icons or a combination of icons and text. Depending on the choice made, this allows us to place between two to five links. This is usually avoided on tablet designs:

An example of classic bottom navigation

- The navigation drawer, opened from the side of the screen. This contains a list of links, possibly more than five. This can be sophisticated and can include a user profile at the top. This tends to be opened by a hamburger icon placed in one of the upper corners:

An example of drawer navigation

- Tabs, which are placed at the top of the screen and appear as pairs, at the least. The number of tabs can exceed four, and in such a case, tabs can be scrolled horizontally. This is used not only for top-level navigation, but for any navigation between screens of the same depth.

Navigating between different levels of the graph

Once we reach a certain level, sometimes we want to explore that particular area even further. In the case of the Tasks application, this would mean choosing a project or choosing a specific task within the project itself.

Usually, to navigate down the graph, we use the following:

- Containers, including lists, cards, image list, and image cards
- Simple buttons, text links, or icons

However, to go back up the graph, usually we use the following:

- A back icon, such as an arrow, usually positioned in the upper left corner or bottom left corner
- A button or link, with text such as **back** | **cancel** | **start over**
- A cross icon positioned in the relevant part of the edit/create screen

To some of you, this knowledge comes naturally; however, I have bumped into proposals or early drafts of designs that clearly confused these concepts and, in the end, terribly affected the user experience. Experimenting is good, but only in a controlled environment that uses standard and well-known patterns, which feel natural for most of the users.

For experimenting with design, you should implement A/B tests. These require the ability to run different versions of the app in production for different subsets of users. Thanks to analytics, you can later assess whether A or B was a better choice. Finally, all of the users can be migrated to the winning scenario.

Navigating on the same level of the graph

In more complex apps, aside from the top-level navigation, you will also need to horizontally transition between different screens that are on the same depth.

To transition between screens on the same level, you can use the following:

- Tabs, similar to that discussed in the top-level navigation section
- Screen swipes (literally swiping between screens)
- Swiping in a container (for instance, to see either task description, connected tasks or task, comments) can be connected with tabs
- Left or right arrows, or dots indicating your position within the level

Similarly, you can use these for collections of data too. Collections of data, however, provide more freedom to use lists or less constrained containers that take advantage of top/bottom swipes, too.

Bearing in mind how designers are solving problems of navigation, let's now discuss how to make it performant and how to maintain the navigation graph.

Developers' navigation patterns

To be honest, it all comes down to this—is a JavaScript implementation good enough? If so, let's use it for our benefit (that is, tracking, control in JavaScript, logs, and so on). Over time, it looks like the React Native community managed to create something stable, called React Navigation:

> *"React Navigation is entirely made up of React components and the state is managed in JavaScript on the same thread as the rest of your app. This is what makes React Navigation great in many ways but it also means that your app logic contends for CPU time with React Navigation — there's only so much JavaScript execution time available per frame."*
> *- React Navigation official documentation, available at:*
> https://reactnavigation.org/docs/en/limitations.html.

However, as discussed in the preceding quote, this competes with your application for CPU cycles. This means it is draining resources and slowing down the application to some extent.

Pros of JavaScript navigation are as follows:

- You can tweak and extend the solution using JavaScript code.
- Current implementations are performant enough for small to medium apps.
- The state is managed in JavaScript and easily integrates with state management libraries such as Redux.

- The API is decoupled from native APIs. This means that if React Native eventually goes beyond Android and iOS, the API will stay the same, and once implemented by the library maintainers, this will enable you to use the same solution for yet another platform.
- Easy to learn.
- Good for beginners.

Cons of JavaScript navigation are as follows:

- It is very tough to implement in a performant way.
- It may still be too slow for large applications.
- Some animations slightly differ from the native ones.
- Some gestures or animations may be entirely different than the native ones (for instance, if the native system changes the defaults, or there is inconsistency because of historical changes).
- It is hard to integrate with native code.
- Routing should be static, as per current documentation.
- Some solutions, which you would expect to be present if you have ever created native navigation, may not be available (for instance, a connection with the native lifecycle).
- Limited international support (for instance, as of July 2018, the Right-to-Left is not supported by some JavaScript navigation libraries, including React Navigation).

On the other hand, let's look at Native navigation.

Pros of Native navigation are as follows:

- Native navigation can be optimized by the system library that may, for instance, containerize navigation stacks
- Native navigation outperforms JavaScript navigation
- It leverages each system's unique capabilities
- The ability to leverage the native life cycle and hook to it with animations
- Most implementations integrate with state management libraries

Cons of Native navigation are as follows:

- Sometimes it defeats React Native's purpose – it diverges navigation across systems, instead unifying it.

- It is tough to provide a consistent API across platforms, or it is even not consistent at all.
- Single source of truth is no longer true – our state leaks to the native code that manages the state internally within the specific platform. This kills time-traveling.
- Problematic state synchronization – the chosen library either does not promise immediate state synchronization at all, or implements different locks that slow down the application to an extent that usually kills the purpose.
  Some experts argue that developers of NavigatorIOS library (as of July 2018, still mentioned in official React Native documentation) did a great job of working on it, but its future is uncertain.
- It requires working with tools and configuration of the native systems.
- It is aimed at experienced developers.

You need to take into account all of this and make the right trade-offs before choosing either one. But before we dive into the code, please focus on the next section.

Restructuring your application

No-one likes huge monolithic code bases with all features intertwined. What can we do to prevent this as the application grows? Make sure to wisely locate code files and have a standardized way of doing so.

An example of a monolithic code base that will cause you a headache once it surpasses 10,000 lines is the following one:

An example of a directory structure that is not good enough for large projects

Imagine one directory with 1,200 reducers to scroll through. You would probably use search instead. Believe me, this also becomes tough with 1,200 reducers.

Instead, it is much better to group code by features. Thanks to this, we will have a clear scope of files to look at while investigating a certain isolated part of the application:

An example of a directory structure that may be good for medium to large projects

To see this new structure in action, please check the code files of `Example 1` from the `src` folder in `Chapter 7`, *Navigation Patterns*.

> If you have ever worked with microservices, think of it as if you wanted your features to be simple micro services within your frontend code base. A screen may ask them to operate by sending data, and expects a certain output.
> In some architectures, every such entity also creates its own Flux store. This is a good separation of concerns for large projects.

React Navigation

Browsers have a navigation solution baked in, React Native needs to have an own one, and there is a reason behind this:

> *"In a web browser, you can link to different pages using an anchor (<a>) tag. When the user clicks on a link, the URL is pushed to the browser history stack. When the user presses the back button, the browser pops the item from the top of the history stack, so the active page is now the previously visited page. React Native doesn't have a built-in idea of a global history stack like a web browser does -- this is where React Navigation enters the story."*
> - React Navigation official documentation, available at:
> `https://reactnavigation.org/docs/en/hello-react-navigation.html.`

To sum this up, our mobile navigation can be handled not only like that seen in a browser, but also in any custom way we please. This is thanks to historical reasons, as some screen changes are usually tied to particular animations that users of the specific operating system do recognize. Thus, it is wise to follow them as closely as possible to resemble the native feel.

Using React Navigation

Let's start our journey with React Navigation by installing the library with the following command:

```
yarn add react-navigation
```

Once the library is installed, let's try the easiest path and use a stack navigation system that resembles the type seen in a browser.

 For those of you who do not know, or have forgotten what a stack is, the name stack comes from a real-life analogy to a set of items stacked on top of each other. Item can be pushed to the stack (placed at the top), or popped from the stack (taken from the top).
A special structure, pushing this idea further, resembles a horizontal stack with access from both the bottom and top. Such a structure is called a queue; however, we will not use queues in this book.

In the previous section, I made a refactor of our file structure. As part of the refactor, I created a new file, called `TaskListScreen`, which is made up of features from our code base:

```
// src / Chapter 7 / Example 2 / src / screens / TaskListScreen.js
export const TaskListScreen = () => (
    <View>
        <AddTaskContainer />      // Please note slight refactor
        <TaskListContainer />     // to two separate containers
    </View>
);

export default withGeneralLayout(TaskListScreen);
```

The `withGeneralLayout` HOC is also part of the refactor and all it does is wrap the screen with a header and bottom bar. Such a wrapped `TaskList` component is ready to be called a `Screen` and be provided straight to the React Navigation setup:

```
// src / Chapter 7 / Example 2 / src / screens / index.js

export default createStackNavigator({
    TaskList: {
        screen: TaskListScrn,
        path: 'project/task/list', // later on:
'project/:projectId/task/list'
        navigationOptions: { header: null }
    },
    ProjectList: {
        screen: () => <View><Text>Under construction.</Text></View>,
        path: 'project/:projectId'
    },
    // ...
}, {
    initialRouteName: 'TaskList',
    initialRouteParams: {}
});
```

Here, we use a `createStackNavigator` function that expects two objects:

- An object representing all of the screens that should be handled by this `StackNavigator`. Each of the screens should specify a component that represents this screen and path. You can also use `navigationOptions` to customize your screen. In our case, we do not want the default header bar.
- An object representing the settings of the navigator itself. You probably want to define the initial route name and its parameters.

Having done this, we have finished the hello world of navigation – we have one screen working.

Multiple screens with React Navigation

It's time to add a Task screen to our `StackNavigator`. Use your newly learned syntax and create a placeholder screen for task details. The following is my implementation:

```
// src / Chapter 7 / Example 3 / src / screens / index.js
// ...
Task: {
    screen: () => <View><Text>Under construction.</Text></View>,
    path: 'project/task/:taskId',
    navigationOptions: ({ navigation }) => ({
        title: `Task ${navigation.state.params.taskId} details`
    })
},
// ...
```

This time, I also pass `navigationOptions`, as I want to use the default navigator top bar with a specific title:

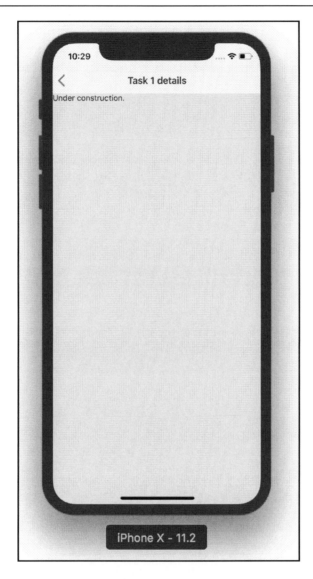

An example of how the new Task screen could look

To navigate to Task Details, we will need a separate link or button that will take us there. Let's create a reusable one in the top of our directory structure, as follows:

```
// src / Chapter 7 / Example 3 / src / components / NavigateButton.js
// ...
export const NavigateButton = ({
    navigation, to, data, text
```

```
    }) => (
        <Button
            onPress={() => navigation.navigate(to, data)}
            title={text}
        />
    );
    // ...
    export default withNavigation(NavigateButton);
```

The last line in the preceding snippet uses the `withNavigation` HOC, which is part of React Navigation. This HOC provides the navigation prop to `NavigateButton`. To, data, and `text` need to be passed manually to the component:

```
// src / Chapter 7 / Example 3 / src / features / tasks / views /
TaskList.js
// ...
<View style={styles.taskText}>
    <Text style={styles.taskName}>
        {task.name}
    </Text>
    <Text>{task.description}</Text>
</View>
<View style={styles.taskActions}>
    <NavigateButton
        data={{ taskId: task.id }}
        to="Task"
        text="Details"
    />
</View>
// ...
```

That's it! Let's look at the following result. Use your skills from Chapter 3, *Styling Patterns*, if you feel the design needs a little polish:

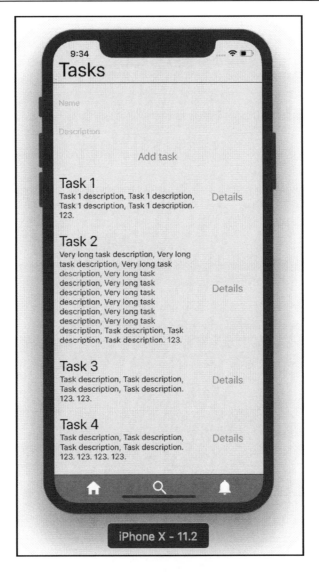

Each Task row is now displaying a Details link

You can now tap the **Details** button to navigate to the Task Details screen.

Tab navigation

As we already have the bottom icon controls in place, it will be very straightforward to make them work. This is a classic example for tab navigation:

```
// src / Chapter 7 / Example 4 / src / screens / index.js
export default createBottomTabNavigator(
    {
        Home: createStackNavigator({
            TaskList: {
                // ...
            },
            // ...
        }, {
            // ...
        }),
        Search: () => (
            <View>
                <Text>Search placeholder. Under construction.</Text>
            </View>
        ),
        Notifications: () => (
            <View>
                <Text>Notifications placeholder. Under construction.</Text>
            </View>
        )
    },
    {
        initialRouteName: 'Home',
        initialRouteParams: {}
    }
);
```

Please note the use of shorthand for creating screens. Instead of using an object, I pass the component directly:

By default, React Navigation will create a bottom bar for us

To disable the bar, we need to pass the appropriate prop, as shown here:

```
// src / Chapter 7 / Example 4 / src / screens / index.js
// ...
{
    initialRouteName: 'Home',
    initialRouteParams: {},
    navigationOptions: () => ({
        tabBarVisible: false
    })
}
```

```
    }
    // ...
```

Now, we need to make our icons respond to a user's touch. First, create a `NavigateIcon` component that you can reuse in your app. Check the repository for a full code sample, but an example is provided here:

```
// src / Chapter 7 / Example 4 / src / components / NavigateIcon.js
export const NavigateIcon = ({
    navigation, to, data, ...iconProps
}) => (
    <Ionicons
        {...iconProps}
        onPress={() => navigation.navigate(to, data)}
    />
);
// ...
export default withNavigation(NavigateIcon);
```

It is fairly straightforward to replace existing icons with the `NavigateIcon`, as shown here:

```
// src / Chapter 7 / Example 4 / src / layout / views / GeneralAppView.js
import NavIonicons from '../../components/NavigateIcon';
<View style={styles.footer}>
    <NavIonicons
        to="Home"
        // ...
    />
    <NavIonicons
        to="Search"
        // ...
    />
    <NavIonicons
        to="Notifications"
        // ...
    />
</View>
```

The last thing to take care of is the general layout. The `Search` and `Notifications` screens should display our custom bottom navigation. This is surprisingly easy thanks to the HOC pattern we have learned:

```
// src / Chapter 7 / Example 4 / src / screens / index.js
// ...
Search: withGeneralLayout(() => (
    <View>
        <Text>Search placeholder. Under construction.</Text>
    </View>
```

```
    )),
    Notifications: withGeneralLayout(() => (
        <View>
            <Text>Notifications placeholder. Under construction.</Text>
        </View>
    ))
    // ...
```

The results are shown in the following screenshot:

The Search screen with its placeholder.

Please fix the header name by adding a configuration object to the `withGeneralLayout` HOC.

Drawer navigation

It's time to implement drawer navigation to allow users to access less commonly used screens, as shown here:

```
// src / Chapter 7 / Example 5 / src / screens / index.js
// ...
export default createDrawerNavigator({
    Home: TabNavigation,
    Profile: withGeneralLayout(() => (
        <View>
            <Text>Profile placeholder. Under construction.</Text>
        </View>
    )),
    Settings: withGeneralLayout(() => (
        <View>
            <Text>Settings placeholder. Under construction.</Text>
        </View>
    ))
});
```

As we have our default drawer ready, let's add an icon which will show it. The hamburger icon is the most popular, and is usually placed within one of the header corners:

```
// src / Chapter 7 / Example 5 / src / layout / views / MenuView.js
const Hamburger = props => (<Ionicons
    onPress={() => props.navigation.toggleDrawer()}
    name="md-menu"
    size={32}
    color="black"
/>);
// ...

const MenuView = withNavigation(Hamburger);
```

Now, just place it in the header part of the `GeneralAppView` component and style it appropriately:

```
// src / Chapter 7 / Example 5 / src / layout / views / GeneralAppView.js
<View style={styles.header}>
    // ...
    <View style={styles.headerMenuIcon}>
```

```
            <MenuView />
        </View>
    </View>
```

That's it, our drawer is fully functional. Your drawer might look something like this:

Opened drawer menu on the iPhone X simulator.

You can open the drawer by clicking the hamburger icon in the upper right corner.

Issues with duplicated data

The task list component fetches the data necessary to display the list on its successful mounting. However, there is no mechanism implemented to prevent duplication of data. This book is not meant to provide recipes for common problems. However, let's think of a few solutions you could implement:

- Change the API and rely on unique task identifiers (such as ID, UUID, or GUID). Make sure you filter to only allow unique ones.
- Clear data on every request. This is good; however, in our case we would lose unsaved (API-related) tasks.
- Maintain status, and only request once. This would work in our simple use case only. In more complex apps, you will need to update data more often.

Okay, bearing this in mind, let's finally dive into the library based on a native navigation solution.

React Native Navigation

In this section, we will play with a native solution for navigation. React Native Navigation is a wrapper on the native navigation for Android and iOS.

Our goal is to recreate what we have achieved in the previous section, but with React Navigation.

A few words on the setup

One of the biggest challenges you may face in this section is setting up the library. Please follow the most up-to-date installation instructions. Take your time—it may take over 8 hours if you are not familiar with the tools and ecosystem.

Follow the installation instructions at the following link: `https://github.com/wix/react-native-navigation`.

> This book uses the API from version 2 of React Native Navigation. To use the same code examples, you will need to install version 2 too.

You may also need to either eject Create React Native App, or bootstrap another project with `react-native init` and copy the key files there. If you struggle with the process, try using the code from `src/Chapter 7/Example 6/` (just React Native) or `src/Chapter 7/Example 7/` (the whole React Native Navigation setup). I used `react-native init` and copied all of the important stuff there.

There will be certainly errors on your path to a working setup. Don't get upset; search for any errors on StackOverflow or GitHub issues with React Native and React Native Navigation.

Basics of React Native Navigation

The first big change is the lack of the `AppRegistry` and the `registerComponent` call. Instead, we will use `Navigation.setRoot(...)` and it will do the job. The `setRoot` function should only be invoked if we are certain that the application was launched successfully, as shown here:

```
// src / Chapter 7 / Example 7 / src / screens / index.js
import { Navigation } from 'react-native-navigation';
// ...
export default () => Navigation.events().registerAppLaunchedListener(() =>
{
    Navigation.setRoot({
        // ...
    });
});
```

Our root/entry file will then only invoke the React Native Navigation function:

```
import start from './src/screens/index';

export default start();
```

Okay. The more interesting part is what we put into the `setRoot` function. Basically, we have a choice here: either stack navigation or tab navigation. Following our previous application, the top-level one will be tab navigation (drawer navigation is decoupled in React Native Navigation).

 At the time of writing this book, using the default built-in bottom bar is the only option to retain previous capabilities. Once library authors release version 2 of RNN and fix `Navigation.mergeOptions(...)`, you will be able to implement custom bottom bars.

First, let's remove the default top bar and customize the bottom bar:

```
// src / Chapter 7 / Example 7 / src / screens / index.js
// ...
Navigation.setRoot({
    root: {
        bottomTabs: {
            children: [
            ],
            options: {
                topBar: {
                    visible: false,
                    drawBehind: true,
                    animate: false
                },
                bottomTabs: {
                    animate: true
                }
            }
        }
    }
});
```

Having done that, we are ready to define the tabs. The very first thing to do in React Native Navigation is register the screens:

```
// src / Chapter 7 / Example 7 / src / screens / index.js
// ...
Navigation.registerComponent(
    'HDPRN.TabNavigation.TaskList',
    () => TaskStackNavigator, store, Provider
);
Navigation.registerComponent(
    'HDPRN.TabNavigation.SearchScreen',
    () => SearchScreen, store, Provider
);
Navigation.registerComponent(
    'HDPRN.TabNavigation.NotificationsScreen',
    () => NotificationsScreen, store, Provider
);
```

When we have all of the basic three screens registered, we can proceed with tab definitions, as follows:

```
// src / Chapter 7 / Example 7 / src / screens / index.js
// ...
children: [
    {
```

```
            stack: {
                id: 'HDPRN.TabNavigation.TaskListStack',
                // TODO: Check below, let's handle this separately
            }
        },
        {
            component: {
                id: 'HDPRN.TabNavigation.SearchScreen',
                name: 'SearchScreen',
                options: {
                    bottomTab: {
                        text: 'Search',
                        // Check sources if you want to know
                        // how to get this icon variable
                        icon: search
                    }
                }
            }
        },
        // Notifications config object omitted: similar as for Search
]
```

We define every single tab out of the three – Tasks, Search, and Notifications. With regard to Tasks, this is another navigator. The Stack navigator can be configured as follows:

```
stack: {
    id: 'HDPRN.TabNavigation.TaskListStack',
    children: [{
        component: {
            id: 'HDPRN.TabNavigation.TaskList',
            name: 'HDPRN.TabNavigation.TaskList',
        }
    }],
    options: {
        bottomTab: {
            text: 'Tasks',
            icon: home
        }
    }
}
```

In the preceding snippet, the `bottomTab` options set the text and icon in the bottom bar:

The Tasks tab with React Native Navigation

Further investigation

I'll leave the investigation of how to implement navigation elements, such as the Drawer or Task Detail screens, to those of you who are brave enough. At the time of writing, React Native Navigation v2 is quite unstable and I chose not to publish any more snippets from this library. For most readers, this should be enough to get the overall feeling.

Summary

In this chapter, we finally expanded our application with far more views than before. You have learned different approaches to navigation in mobile applications. In the React Native world, it is either native navigation, JavaScript navigation, or a hybrid of the two. Along with learning navigation itself, we have used components including `StackNavigation`, `TabNavigation`, and `DrawerNavigation`.

For the first time, we have also ejected the Create React Native App and installed native code from the native navigation library. We are starting to dive really deeply into React Native. Now is the time to step back and refresh our JavaScript knowledge. We will learn patterns that are not only beneficial in React Native, but in JavaScript overall.

Further reading

- React Navigation common mistakes – from the official documentation, available at:

  `https://reactnavigation.org/docs/en/common-mistakes.html.`

- Thousand ways to navigate in React Native, by Charles Mangwa:

  `https://www.youtube.com/watch?v=d11dGHVVahk.`

- Navigation playground for React Navigation:

  `https://expo.io/@react-navigation/NavigationPlayground.`

- Expo documentation on navigation:

  `https://docs.expo.io/versions/v29.0.0/guides/routing-and-navigation.`

- Material Design on Tabs:

  `https://material.io/design/components/tabs.html#placement.`

- Section on Navigation within the Awesome React Native repository:

  `https://github.com/jondot/awesome-react-native#navigation.`

8
JavaScript and ECMAScript Patterns

In this chapter, we will go back to the heart of the JavaScript language. Some of the patterns here can be reused across many different languages, such as Java, C++, and Python. It is vital to fill your toolbox with such powerful things. This time, we will implement well-known design patterns in JavaScript and see how we can benefit from them, especially within the React Native environment. As a little addition, we will learn a new library, called Ramda, which is known for its great functionalities that can help us to write much shorter and concise code. You will also get to know the fundamentals of functional programming, which will be the topic of the next chapter.

In this chapter, you will learn about the following:

- Selector patterns
- Currying patterns
- The Ramda library
- Basics of functional programming

JavaScript and functional programming

Functional programming basically means using functions in a certain way to write a logical piece of code. Most languages allow functions to be really complex and hard to understand. Functional programming, however, puts constraints on functions in order to be able to compose them and mathematically prove something about their behaviour.

One of the constraints is the regulation of communication with the external world (for instance, side effects, such as data fetching). Some assert that no matter how many times we call a function with the same arguments, it will return the exact same value. All of these constraints will give us certain benefits. You can name some of these benefits already, such as time-traveling, which uses pure reducers.

In this chapter, we will learn a bunch of useful functions that will ease us into `Chapter 9, Elements of Functional Programming Patterns`. We will also elaborate more on the exact constraints and their benefits.

ES6 map, filter, and reduce

This section is aimed at refreshing our knowledge on the `map`, `filter`, and `reduce` functions.

 Usually, common language functions need to be extremely performant, which is a topic that spans beyond this book. Avoid reimplementing what is in the language already. Some of the examples in this chapter are here only for learning purposes.

`reduce` is most likely often neglected, hence, we will focus on it. Usually, `reduce` (as the name suggests) is used to reduce a collection in size to a smaller one, or even a single variable.

Here is the reduce function declaration:

```
reduce(callback, [initialValue])
```

The callback takes four arguments: `previousValue`, `currentValue`, `index`, and `array`.

To quickly remind you how the `reduce` function works, let's look at the following example:

```
const sumArrayElements = arr => arr.reduce((acc, elem) => acc+elem, 0);
console.log(sumArrayElements([5,15,20])); // 40
```

`reduce` iterates over the collection. At each step, it calls the function on the element iterator it is at. Then it remembers the function output and passes to the next element. This remembered output is the first function argument; in the preceding example, it is the accumulator (`acc`) variable. It remembers the result of the previously run function, applies the `reducer` function and passes along to the following step. This is very similar to how the Redux library operates on the state.

The second argument of the `reduce` function is the initial value of the accumulator; in the preceding example, we start with zero.

Let's rise the bar and implement an `average` function using `reduce`:

```
const numbers = [1, 2, 5, 7, 13];
const average = numbers.reduce(
    (accumulator, currNumber, indexOfElProcessed, arrayWeWorkOn) => {
        // Sum all numbers so far
        const newAcc = accumulator + currNumber;
        if (indexOfElProcessed === arrayWeWorkOn.length - 1) {
            // if this is the last item, return average
            return newAcc / arrayWeWorkOn.length;
        }
        // if not the last item, pass sum
        return newAcc;
    },
    0
);
// average equals 5.6
```

In this example, we do a trick with the `if` statement. If the element is the last one in the array, then we want to calculate `average` instead of the `sum`.

Using reduce to reimplement filter and map

It's time for a little challenge. Did you know that you can implement both `map` and `filter` with `reduce`?

Before we begin, let's do a quick recap how the `filter` function works:

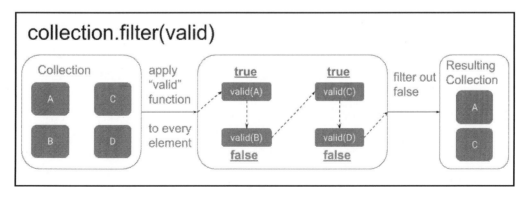

How the filter function works on collection

Suppose we have a `task` collection and want to filter only tasks with `type` equal to 1, as follows:

```
const onlyType1 = task => task.type === 1
```

With a standard filter function, you would simply write the following:

```
tasks.filter(onlyType1)
```

But now, imagine there was no `filter` function and, so far, you only had `reduce` in your toolbox.

You could do the following:

```
tasks.reduce((acc,t) => onlyType1(t) ? [...acc, t] :acc, [])
```

The trick is to make the accumulator into a collection. The previous value is always a collection, starting from the empty array. Step by step, we either add tasks to the accumulator or simply return the accumulator if the task fails to pass the filter.

What about implementing the `map` function? `map` just transforms each element into a new element by applying a mapping function that is passed to it:

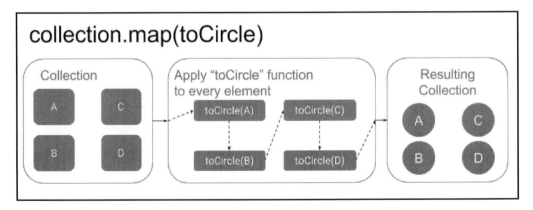

How the map function works on collection

Let's do it using `reduce`, as follows:

```
const someFunc = x => x+1;
const tab = [1, 5, 9, 13];
tab.reduce((acc, elem) => [...acc, someFunc(elem)], []);
// result: [2, 6, 10, 14]
```

In this example, we just collect every item again into the same collection, but before adding it into the array, we apply a mapping function on it. In this example, the mapping function is defined under the name `someFunc`.

Counting items in an array

Our next example is about counting the items in an array. Let's say you have an array of house items. You need to count how many of each you own. Using the `reduce` function, the expected outcome is an object with items as keys and a count of particular items as values, as follows:

```
const items = ['fork', 'laptop', 'fork', 'chair', 'bed', 'knife', 'chair'];
items.reduce((acc, elem) => ({ ...acc, [elem]: (acc[elem] || 0) + 1 }),
{});
// {fork: 2, laptop: 1, chair: 2, bed: 1, knife: 1}
```

This is quite tricky: the part `(acc[elem] || 0)` means we either take the value of `acc[elem]`, if it is defined, or otherwise, 0. This way, we check for the first element of its kind. Also, `{ [elem]: something }` is syntax used to define a key with the name that is stored in the `elem` variable.

> The preceding example is helpful when you work with serialized data that came from an external API. Sometimes you need to transform it in order to cache it, so it avoids unnecessary re-rendering.

The next example introduces a new word—**flattening**. When we flatten a collection, it means it is a nested collection in a collection and we want it to make it flat.

For instance, a collection such as `[[1, 2, 3], [4, 5, 6], [7, 8, 9]]` becomes `[1, 2, 3, 4, 5, 6, 7, 8, 9]` after flattening. This is done as follows:

```
const numCollections = [[1, 2, 3], [4, 5, 6], [7, 8, 9]];
numCollections.reduce((acc, collection) => [...acc, ...collection], []);
// result:[1, 2, 3, 4, 5, 6, 7, 8, 9]
```

This example is essential to understand flattening in the more complex examples that we will use in `Chapter 9`, *Elements of Functional Programming Patterns*.

The iterator pattern

In the previous section, we traversed many different collections, even nested ones. Now, it's time to learn more about the iterator pattern. This pattern especially shines if you plan to use the Redux Saga library.

 If you jumped straight to this chapter, I highly advise you to read the section that introduces iterator patterns in Chapter 6, *Data Transfer Patterns*. That chapter also covers the Redux Saga library and generators.

To recap, in JavaScript, an iterator is an object that knows how to traverse items of a collection one at a time. It must expose the next() function, which returns the next item of a collection. The collection can be whatever it wants. It can even be an infinite collection, such as the Fibonacci numbers, as seen here:

```
class FibonacciIterator {
    constructor() {
        this.n1 = 1;
        this.n2 = 1;
    }
    next() {
        var current = this.n2;
        this.n2 = this.n1;
        this.n1 = this.n1 + current;
        return current;
    }
}
```

Before you can use this, you need to create an instance of a class:

```
const fibNums = new FibonacciIterator();
fibNums.next(); // 1
fibNums.next(); // 1
fibNums.next(); // 2
fibNums.next(); // 3
fibNums.next(); // 5
```

This could quickly get boring, as it smells like an academic example. But it is not. It is useful to show you the algorithm with which we will recreate with closure and the Symbol iterator.

Defining a custom iterator

As a quick recap on symbols in JavaScript: `CallingSymbol()` returns a unique symbol value. A symbol value should be treated as an ID, for instance, as an ID to be used as a key in an object.

To define an iterator for a collection, you need to specify the special key, `Symbol.iterator`. If such a symbol is defined, we say that the collection is iterable. See the following:

```
// Array is iterable by default,
// we don't need to create a custom iterator,
// just use the one that is present.
const alpha = ['a','b','c'];
const it = alpha[Symbol.iterator]();

it.next();   //{ value: 'a', done: false }
it.next();   //{ value: 'b', done: false }
it.next();   //{ value: 'c', done: false }
it.next();   //{ value: undefined, done: true }
```

Let's now create a custom `iterator` for the Fibonacci collection. The Fibonacci sequence is characterized by the fact that every number after the first two is the sum of the two preceding ones (the beginning of the sequence is 1, 1, 2, 3, 5, 8, 13, 21, 34, 55, 89, 144, ...):

```
const fib = {
    [Symbol.iterator]() {
        let n1 = 1;
        let n2 = 1;

        return {
            next() {
                const current = n2;
                n2 = n1;
                n1 += current;
                return { value: current, done: false };
            },

            return(val) { // this part handles loop break
                // Fibonacci sequence stopped.
                return { value: val, done: true };
            }
        };
    }
};
```

To easily traverse iterable collections, we can use the handy `for...of` loop:

```
for (const num of fib) {
    console.log(num);
    if (num > 70) break; // We do not want to iterate forever
}
```

Using generators as a factory for iterators

We will also need to know how to use generators (for instance, for Redux Saga), so we should get fluent in writing them. It turns out they can act like a factory for the iterators that we have learned already.

A quick recap on generators—they are functions with `*` and `yield` operators within their scope, such as, `function* minGenExample() { yield "a"; }`. Such functions execute until the `yield` keyword is encountered. Then, the function returns with the `yield` value. Functions can have many `yields`, and on their first call, return `Generator`. Such a generator is iterable. Look at the following:

```
const a = function* gen() { yield "a"; };
console.log(a.prototype)
// Generator {}
```

We can now use this knowledge to reimplement Fibonacci as a generator:

```
function* fib() {
    let n1 = 1;
    let n2 = 1;
    while (true) {
        const current = n2;
        n2 = n1;
        n1 += current;

        yield current;
    }
}
// Pay attention to invocation of fib to get Generator
for (const num of fib()) {
    console.log(num);
    if (num > 70) break;
}
```

That's it. We used generator function syntax to simplify things for ourselves. The generator function is like a factory for iterators. Once invoked, it will provide you with a new generator that you can iterate over like any other collection.

The piece of code that handles Fibonacci numbers can be simplified. The shortest way I could write this is as follows:

```
function* fib() {
  let n1 = 1, n2 = 1;
  while (true) {
    yield n1;
    [n1, n2] = [n2, n1 + n2];
  }
}
```

Making an API call to fetch task details with a generator

We have already tried generators and we have successfully fetched tasks using them. Now, we will repeat the process, but with a slightly different goal: to fetch the data of a single task. To achieve this, I have made a few changes to the code base and prepared the parts of code to keep your eyes on generators only:

```
// src/Chapter 8/Example 1/src/features/tasks/sagas/fetchTask.js
// ^ fully functional example with TaskDetails page
export function* fetchTask(action) {
    const task = yield call(apiFetch, `tasks/${action.payload.taskId}`);
    if (task.error) {
        yield put(ActionCreators.fetchTaskError(task.error));
    } else {
        const json = yield call([task.response, 'json']);
        yield put(ActionCreators.fetchTaskComplete(json));
    }
}
```

This generator takes care of the API call first. The endpoint is calculated using the payload from a dispatched action. A string template is used for convenience. Then, based on the outcome, we either dispatch a success action or an error action:

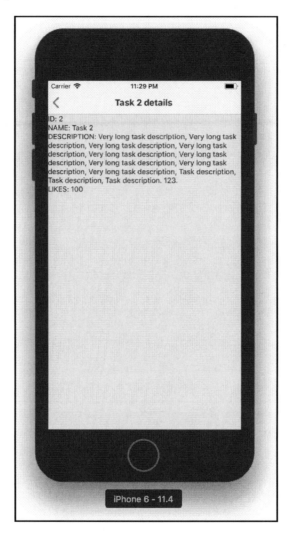

This is an example of the Task Details screen. Feel free to work on the styles.

Please pay attention to the numerous yields in the generator. We stop function execution with every yield. In our example, the execution is resumed on a finished `call` effect. Then, we can proceed, knowing the result of the call.

But why would we want to stop? Is there any use case for this? First of all, it's more powerful than simple promises and async/await (there will be more on this in the following section). Secondly, it is handy to stop and wait for certain things to happen. Imagine, for example, that we want to wait until the creation of three tasks to display a congratulations message, as seen here:

```
function* watchFirstThreeTasksCreation() {
    for (let i = 0; i < 3; i++) {
        const action = yield take(TasksActionTypes.ADD_TASK)
    }
    yield put({type: 'SHOW__THREE_TASKS_CONGRATULATION'})
}
```

This example is for playground purposes only. Pay attention to the fact that the task creation counter is within the generator function. Hence, is not saved in any backend system. On app refresh, the counter will reset. If you build any reward system for your application, keep such issues under consideration.

Alternatives to generators

A popular alternative that has been in JavaScript for years is that of promises. The promises use a very similar concept to generators. The syntactic sugar allows you to await the promise. If you want this syntactic sugar, then your function needs to be `async`. Do you see any similarity? Yeah, I would risk saying that promises are a less powerful variation of generators.

If you do use promises, take a look at a new loop called `for await of`. You may find it handy. Another feature worth checking is **asynchronous iterators**.

Selectors

In the previous section, we worked with async data again. This data has been pushed to the application's Redux store. We have accessed it numerous times in `mapStateToProps` functions, for example, in the task list container:

```
const mapStateToProps = state => ({
    tasks: state.tasks.get('entities'),
    isLoading: state.tasks.get('isLoading'),
```

```
        hasError: state.tasks.get('hasError'),
        errorMsg: state.tasks.get('errorMsg')
});
```

This one is not looking very ugly, but for the task details page, it already is getting out of control. Consider the following:

```
// On this page we don't know if tasks are already fetched
const mapStateToProps = (state, ownProps) => ({
    task: state.tasks
        ? state.tasks
            .get('entities')
            .find(task => task.id === ownProps.taskId)
        : null
});
```

We do numerous checks and then transformations. This flow happens on every re-render. Could we somehow remember the calculations if the data did not change? Yes we can—here come cached selectors to the rescue.

Selecting from the Redux store

Let's face it, we did not have any abstraction on accessing the store so far. This means that every `mapStateToProps` function accessed it on its own. In case of store shape change, all `mapStateToProps` functions could be affected. The first step is to separate the concerns and provide selectors, instead of straightforward object access:

```
// src/Chapter 8/Example 1/src/features/
//                     ./tasks/containers/TaskListContainer.js
const mapStateToProps = state => ({
    tasks: tasksEntitiesSelector(state),
    isLoading: tasksIsLoadingSelector(state),
    hasError: tasksHasErrorSelector(state),
    errorMsg: tasksErrorMsgSelector(state)
});
```

The implementation is just the same as before, with the simple exception that we can reuse the code in many places:

```
// src/Chapter 8/Example 2/src/features/
//                     ./tasks/state/selectors/tasks.js

export const tasksSelector = state => state.tasks;

export const tasksEntitiesSelector = state =>
```

```
    (tasksSelector(state) ? tasksSelector(state).get('entities') : null);

export const tasksIsLoadingSelector = state =>
    (tasksSelector(state) ? tasksSelector(state).get('isLoading') : null);

export const tasksHasErrorSelector = state =>
    (tasksSelector(state) ? tasksSelector(state).get('hasError') : null);

export const tasksErrorMsgSelector = state =>
    (tasksSelector(state) ? tasksSelector(state).get('errorMsg') : null);

// PS: I have refactored the rest of the app to selectors too.
```

Even in this little example, we access `tasksSelector` twice in every other selector. If `tasksSelector` was expensive, it would be really inefficient. However, we will now shield ourselves from such a scenario by caching the selectors.

Caching the selectors

To cache the selector, we will use the **memoization** function. Such a function recomputes the value once the function's input reference changes. To save us time, we will use a popular library that implements this memoization function for us. The library is called `reselect`. In `reselect`, the reference change is checked with strong equality (==), but you can change the equality function to your own if you need. Add the library with the following command:

```
yarn add reselect
```

With that, we are ready to cache:

```
// src/Chapter 8/Example 2/src/features/
//                          ./tasks/state/selectors/tasks.js
import { createSelector } from 'reselect';

export const tasksSelector = state => state.tasks;

export const tasksEntitiesSelector = createSelector(
    tasksSelector,
    tasks => (tasks ? tasks.get('entities') : null)
);

// ... rest of the selectors in similar fashion
```

Learning functions from the Ramda library

Map, filter, reduce, iterators, generators, and selectors. Not too much, right? Don't get too scared, can you speak English using only 10 words? No? Okay, then we can proceed with learning some new words that will make us more fluent in JavaScript programming.

Composing functions

One of the most advertised features of HOCs is their composability. Taking, for instance, the `withLogger`, `withAnalytics`, and `withRouter` HOCs, we can compose them in the following fashion:

```
withLogger(withAnalytics(withRouter(SomeComponent)))
```

The Ramda library takes composability to the next level. Unfortunately, I find many developers hardly understand it. Let's look at an equivalent example:

```
R.compose(withLogger,withAnalytics, withRouter)(SomeComponent)
```

What most people find hard about Ramda `compose` is understanding how it works. It generally applies functions from right to left, meaning that it first evaluates `withRouter` and then forwards results to `withAnalytics`, and so on. The most important thing about the functions is that only the first one (`withRouter`) can have multiple arguments. Every following function needs to operate on the result of the previous one.

 The Ramda `compose` function composes functions from right to left. To compose functions from left to right you can use the Ramda `pipe` function.

The importance of this example to your React or React Native code base is the fact that you don't need `reselect` or any other library to compose things. You can do it on your own. This will come in handy in use cases such as the `reselect` library, which expects you to compose selectors. Spend some time getting used to it.

Fighting the confusing code

The next interesting pattern I see in code written by skilled Ramda users is so-called **pointfree** code. It means there is only one single place where we pass all data. As beautiful as it sounds, I wouldn't recommend you to be so strict about it. But there is a nice thing we can derive from this approach.

Consider refactoring your code from this:

```
const myHoc = SomeComponent => R.compose(withLogger,withAnalytics,
withRouter)(SomeComponent)
```

You could refactor it to this:

```
const myHoc = R.compose(withLogger,withAnalytics, withRouter)
```

This will hide the obvious part. The most common problem is that it starts to act like a magic box, where only we know how to pass data to it. If you use a type system such as TypeScript or Flow, it will be much easier to quickly look it up if you have no idea. But, surprisingly, many developers will freak out at this point. The less they understand about how `compose` works (particularly the right to left function application), the more likely they will have no idea what to pass to this function.

Consider this:

```
const TaskNamesList = tasks => tasks
    .map({ name }) => (
        <View><Text>{name}</Text></View>
    ))
```

Now compare the previous example to this freak version of `compose`:

```
const TaskComponent = name => (<View><Text>{name}</Text></View>)

const TaskNamesList = compose(
    map(TaskComponent),
    map(prop('name')) // prop function maps object to title key
);
```

In the first example, you will probably be able to understand what is happening in less than 30 seconds. In the second example, it may take over one minute for a beginner to understand the code. This is unacceptable.

Currying functions

Okay, bearing in mind the challenges from the previous section, let's now focus on the other side of a coin. In brownfield applications, we may bump into the problem that it is very risky or time-consuming to modify a function that we would like to use in a different way.

Brownfield applications are applications that were developed in the past and are fully functional. Some of these applications may be built using old patterns or approaches. We cannot usually afford to rewrite them to the latest trend, such as React Native. If they are battle-tested, why would we even bother? Hence, we will need to find a way to connect both worlds if we decide that a new trend will give us enough of a benefit by switching to it for its new features.

Imagine a function that expects you to pass two parameters, but you would like to pass one, and then the other later on:

```
const oldFunc = (x, y) => { // something }

const expected = x => y => { // something }
```

This is tricky if you don't want to modify the function. However, we could write a `util` function that would do this for us:

```
const expected = x => y => oldFunc(x, y)
```

Awesome. But why bother to write a helper in every such case? It's time to introduce `curry`:

```
const notCurriedFunc = (x, y, z) => x + y + z;

const curriedFunc = R.curry(notCurriedFunc);

// Usage: curriedFunc(a)(b)(c)
// or shorter: R.curry(notCurriedFunc)(a)(b)(c)


// So our case with partial application could be:
const first = R.curry(notCurriedFunc)(a)(b);
// ... <pass it somewhere else where c will be present> ...
const final = first(c)
```

That's it. We made it behave just like we wanted, and we didn't even change a single line in the brownfield app function (`oldFunc` or `notCurriedFunc`).

If there are only one or two places in your app where you would use `curry`, think twice. Will there be more use cases in the future? If not, it is probably overkill to use it. Use the helper arrow functions, as shown previously.

Flipping

It is nice that we can `curry` a function, but what if we wanted to pass arguments in a different sequence? For the change of the first two arguments, there is a handy function called `flip`, demonstrated here:

```
const someFunc = x => y => z => x + y + z;

const someFuncYFirst = R.flip(someFunc);
// equivalent to (y => x => z => x + y + z;)
```

If we needed to reverse all of the arguments, unfortunately there is no such function. But we can write it out nonetheless for our use case:

```
const someFuncReverseArgs = z => y => x => someFunc(x, y, z);
```

Summary

In this chapter, we dived into the world of different patterns that are commonly found in modern JavaScript, such as iterators, generators, useful reduce use cases, selectors, and function composition.

You have also learnt a handful of functions from the Ramda library. Ramda deserves much more attention than a few pages of simple use cases. Please have a look at it in your free time.

In the next chapter, we will use what we have learned here to look at functional programming and its benefits.

Further reading

- Iterators and generators article in the Mozilla guide:

  ```
  https://developer.mozilla.org/en-US/docs/Web/JavaScript/Guide/
  Iterators_and_Generators.
  ```

- Reselect documentation FAQ:

  ```
  https://github.com/reduxjs/reselect#faq.
  ```

- Old-school design patterns that are not only used in JavaScript:

  `https://medium.com/@tkssharma/js-design-patterns-quick-look-fbc9ebfaf9aa.`

- TC39 proposal for asynchronous iterators for JavaScript:

  `https://github.com/tc39/proposal-async-iteration.`

9
Elements of Functional Programming Patterns

This is an advanced chapter that focuses on the functional programming paradigm and design patterns that come from the functional programming world. It is high time to dive deep into why we have the option of creating stateless and stateful components. This comes down to understanding what pure functions are and how immutable objects help us to predict application behavior. Once we have clarified that, we will move on to higher-order functions and higher-order components. You have used them already many times, but this time we will look at them from a slightly different perspective.

Throughout this book, I have challenged you with many concepts that will get much much clearer after reading this chapter. I hope you will embrace them in your applications and use them wisely, keeping in mind the maturity of your team. These patterns are good to know but are not essential to either React or React Native development. However, at some point when reading pull requests to the React or React Native repositories, you will find yourself referring back to this chapter quite often.

In this chapter, we will cover the following topics:

- Mutable and immutable structures
- Specific functions, such as pure functions
- `Maybe` monad and the monad pattern
- Functional programming benefits
- Caching and memorization

Mutable and immutable objects

This concept surprised me in one of my coding interviews. At the beginning of my career, I had little knowledge of mutable and immutable objects and it backfired without me even realizing the root cause.

In `Chapter 5`, *Store Patterns*, I explained the basics of mutability and immutability. We even used the `Immutable.js` library. That part of the book was heavily focused on the store. Now let's look at the bigger picture. Why do we even need mutable or immutable objects?

Usually, the main reason is the ability to quickly reason about our application's behavior. For instance, React wants to quickly check whether it should re-render components. If you create object *A* and you are guaranteed that it won't ever change, then to reassure yourself that nothing changed, the only thing you need to do is compare the reference to the object. If it is the same as before, then object *A* remained unchanged. If object *A* could change, we would need to compare every single nested key within object *A* to be sure it remained unchanged. If object *A* had nested objects and we wanted to know whether those did not change, we would need to repeat the process for the nested objects. This is a lot of work, especially as object *A* grows. But why would we need to do it this way?

Immutable primitives in JavaScript

In JavaScript, primitive data types (number, string, Boolean, undefined, null, and symbol) are immutable. Objects are mutable. In addition, JavaScript is loosely typed; that means the variable does not need to be of a certain type. For instance, you may declare variable A and assign the number 5 to it, and then later decide to assign an object to it. JavaScript allows that.

To simplify things, the community has created two very important movements:

- Libraries that guarantee immutability of objects
- Static type-checkers for JavaScript, such as Flow or TypeScript

The first one provides functions to create objects that guarantee their immutability. This means that, whenever you want to change something within an object, it will clone itself, apply the change, and return a brand new immutable object.

The second, static type-checkers, primarily solves the problem of human error when developers accidentally try to assign a value of a different type than initially expected. Hence, if you declare `variableA` to be a number, you can never assign a string to it. To us, it means type immutability. If you want a different type, you need to create a new variable and map `variableA` to it.

 An important side note on the `const` keyword: `const` operates on the reference level. It forbids a reference change. The value of a constant variable cannot be reassigned and cannot be redeclared. With primitive immutable types, it simply means freezing them for life. You can never reassign a new value to the variable. Trying to assign a different value will also fail, because primitives are immutable and it simply means creating a brand new reference. With objects that are mutable types, it simply means freezing the object reference. We cannot reassign a new object to the variable, but we can change the contents of the object. This means we can mutate what is inside. This is not very useful.

Immutability cost explained

When I was first introduced to this concept, I started to scratch my head. How is it any faster? If you want to modify an object, you need to clone it and this is a serious cost with any simple change. I thought it was unacceptable. I assumed it was the same cost as if we were performing equality check on every level. I was both right and wrong.

It depends on the tools you use. Special data structures, such as Immutable.js, make numerous optimizations to work easily. However, if you clone your objects with the `spread` operator or `Object.assign()`, then you recreate the whole object again or unknowingly just clone one level deep.

> *"For deep cloning, we need to use other alternatives because Object.assign() copies property values. If the source value is a reference to an object, it only copies that reference value."*
> *- Mozilla JavaScript Documentation*
> ```
> https://developer.mozilla.org/en-US/docs/Web/JavaScript/Reference/
> Global_Objects/Object/assign.
> ```

> *"Spread syntax effectively goes one level deep while copying an array. Therefore, it may be unsuitable for copying multidimensional arrays [...] (it's the same with Object.assign() and spread syntax)."*
> *- Mozilla JavaScript Documentation*
> ```
> https://developer.mozilla.org/pl/docs/Web/JavaScript/Reference/
> Operators/Spread_syntax.
> ```

This is very convenient and we abuse this fact many times in React apps. Let's look at this with an example. The following is the object we will perform operations on:

```
const someObject = {
    x: "1",
    y: 2,
    z: {
        a: 1,
        b: 2,
        c: {
            x1: 1,
            x2: 2
        }
    }
};
```

First, we will clone just one level deep, and then mutate something two levels deep in the cloned object. Observe what happens to the original object:

```
function naiveSpreadClone(obj) { // objects are passed by reference
    return { ...obj };
    // copy one level deep ( nested z cloned by reference )
}
const someObject2 = naiveSpreadClone(someObject); // invoke func
someObject2.z.a = 10; // mutate two levels deep
console.log(someObject2.z.a); // logs 10
console.log(someObject.z.a); // logs 10
// nested object in original someObject mutated too!
```

This is one of the gotchas of mutations. If you are not proficient enough to understand what is going on, you may generate bugs that are incredibly hard to fix. The question is, how do we clone two levels deep? See the following:

```
function controlledSpreadClone(obj) {
    return { ...obj, z: { ...obj.z } }; // copy 2 levels deep
}

const someObject2 = controlledSpreadClone(someObject);
someObject2.z.a = 10; // mutation only in copied object
console.log(someObject2.z.a); // logs 10
console.log(someObject.z.a); // logs 1
```

If you need to, you may use this technique to copy the whole object this way.

 Copying just one level deep is often called a **shallow copy**.

Benchmark on read/write operations

To better understand the tradeoffs and which library to decide on for your specific use case, please have a look at the read and write operations benchmarks. This should serve as a general idea. Please run your own tests before making the final call.

I have used the benchmarks created by ImmutableAssign authors. The code automatically compares numerous libraries and approaches to solve immutability in JavaScript.

First, let's look at pure JavaScript with just simple mutable structures. We do not care about any benefits, just use them as is for a benchmark:

Nearly-new MacBook Pro 15" (2018) with no background tasks	MacBook Pro 15" (2016) with a few background tasks running
Mutable objects and arrays Object: read (x500000): 9 ms Object: write (x100000): 3 ms Object: very deep read (x500000): 31 ms Object: very deep write (x100000): 9 ms Object: merge (x100000): 17 ms Array: read (x500000): 4 ms Array: write (x100000): 3 ms Array: deep read (x500000): 5 ms Array: deep write (x100000): 2 ms Total elapsed 49 ms (read) + **17 ms (write)** + 17 ms (merge) = 83 ms.	**Mutable objects and arrays** Object: read (x500000): 11 ms Object: write (x100000): 4 ms Object: very deep read (x500000): 42 ms Object: very deep write (x100000): 12 ms Object: merge (x100000): 17 ms Array: read (x500000): 7 ms Array: write (x100000): 3 ms Array: deep read (x500000): 7 ms Array: deep write (x100000): 3 ms Total elapsed 67 ms (read) + **22 ms (write)** + 17 ms (merge) = 106 ms.

In the parentheses, you can see a number of performed operations. It is incredibly fast. No immutable solution can outperform this benchmark, as it uses just mutable JS objects and arrays.

Some things to spot are differences based on how deep we read. For instance, the object read (x500000) takes 11 ms, while the very deep object read (x500000) takes 42 ms, which is nearly 4x longer:

Nearly-new MacBook Pro 15" (2018) with no background tasks	MacBook Pro 15" (2016) with a few background tasks running
Immutable objects and arrays (Object.assign) Object: read (x500000): 13 ms Object: write (x100000): 85 ms Object: very deep read (x500000): 30 ms Object: very deep write (x100000): 220 ms Object: merge (x100000): 91 ms Array: read (x500000): 7 ms Array: write (x100000): 402 ms Array: deep read (x500000): 9 ms Array: deep write (x100000): 400 ms Total elapsed 59 ms(read)+**1107 ms(write)**+91 ms(merge) = 1257 ms.	**Immutable objects and arrays (Object.assign)** Object: read (x500000): 19 ms Object: write (x100000): 107 ms Object: very deep read (x500000): 33 ms Object: very deep write (x100000): 255 ms Object: merge (x100000): 136 ms Array: read (x500000): 11 ms Array: write (x100000): 547 ms Array: deep read (x500000): 14 ms Array: deep write (x100000): 504 ms Total elapsed 77 ms(read)+**1413 ms(write)**+136 ms(merge) = 1626 ms.

`Object.assign` creates a spike on write operations. Now we see the cost of copying things that are not needed. The object write operation on a very deep level is close to 25 times more costly. An array deep write is 100 to 200 times slower than the mutable way:

Nearly-new MacBook Pro 15" (2018) with no background tasks	MacBook Pro 15" (2016) with a few background tasks running
Immutable.js objects and arrays	**Immutable.js objects and arrays**
Object: read (x500000): 12 ms	Object: read (x500000): 24 ms
Object: write (x100000): 19 ms	Object: write (x100000): 52 ms
Object: very deep read (x500000): 111 ms	Object: very deep read (x500000): 178 ms
Object: very deep write (x100000): 80 ms	Object: very deep write (x100000): 125 ms
Object: merge (x100000): 716 ms	Object: merge (x100000): 1207 ms
Array: read (x500000): 18 ms	Array: read (x500000): 24 ms
Array: write (x100000): 135 ms	Array: write (x100000): 255 ms
Array: deep read (x500000): 51 ms	Array: deep read (x500000): 128 ms
Array: deep write (x100000): 97 ms	Array: deep write (x100000): 137 ms
Total elapsed	Total elapsed
192 ms(read)+**331 ms(write)**+716 ms(merge) = 1239 ms.	354 ms(read)+**569 ms(write)**+1207 ms(merge) = 2130 ms.

The object write is 6 times slower than the mutable way. A very deep object write is nearly 9 times slower than the mutable way, and 2.75 times faster than with `Object.assign()`. The merge operation, which constructs the object that is a result of merging the two objects passed as arguments, is much slower (42 times slower than a mutable one or even 70 times slower if the user is using other programs).

Please pay attention to the hardware used. It is either a 2016 MacBook Pro or 2018 MacBook Pro, which are both blazing-fast machines. Taking this to the mobile world will spike those benchmarks even more. The purpose of this section is to give you a general idea of how the numbers compare. Before you jump to a conclusion, please run your own tests on a specific hardware relevant to your project.

Pure functions

In this section, we come back to the pure functions that we have already learned, but now from a different perspective. Do you remember that Redux tries to be as explicit as possible? There is a reason for that. Everything that is implicit is usually the root cause of troubles. Do you remember functions from math classes? Those are 100% explicit. There is nothing else happening other than transforming the input into some output.

In JavaScript, however, function can have implicit output. It may change a value, change an external system, and many many other things may happen outside of the function scope. You have already learned that in `Chapter 5`, *Store Patterns*. All such implicit output is usually referred to as side effects.

We need to address all of the different flavours of side effects. One of our weapons is immutability, which shields us from implicit external object changes. This is what immutability is for—it guarantees no such thing ever happens.

In JavaScript, we cannot eliminate all side effects by introducing weapons such as immutability. Some require the tools on the language level, which are not available. In functional programming languages such as Haskell, even input/output is controlled by a separate structure called `IO()`. In JavaScript, however, we need to deal with it on our own. This means we cannot avoid some functions being impure—as those need to take care of API calls.

Another example is randomness. Any function using `Math.random` cannot be considered pure, as some part of such functions rely on the random number generator, which defeats the purpose of pure functions. Once the function is invoked with certain arguments, you are not guaranteed to receive the same output.

Similarly, everything that relies on time is impure. If your function execution relies on the month, day, second, or even year, it cannot be considered a pure function. At some point, the same argument will not give the same output.

In the end, it all comes down to the execution chain. If you want to say a subset of operations were pure, then you need to know that each one of them was pure. An minimalist example is a function that consumes another function:

```
const example = someArray => someFunc => someFunc(someArray);
```

In this example, we do not know what `someFunc` will be. If `someFunc` is impure, the `example` function will also be impure.

Pure functions in Redux

The good news is we can push side-effects to one place of our application and call them in a loop when we really need them. This is what Flux does. Redux embraces it even further, allowing only pure functions as reducers. This is understandable. Reducers are called when the impure part is already done. From there on, we can maintain immutability, at least in terms of the Redux stores.

Some may question whether this is a good choice in terms of performance. Trust me, it is. We have a really low number of events happening (that need to be reduced, and hence affect the store) in comparison with state accesses and selectors operating on the computed state.

In return for keeping the state immutable, we get a huge benefit. We can tell the order of the function application that led to this particular state. We can track it if we really need to. This is huge. We can apply those functions again in a test environment and we will be guaranteed that the output is exactly the same. This is thanks to the functions being pure—hence, no side-effects are generated.

Caching pure functions

Caching is a technique of remembering computations. If you are guaranteed that for certain arguments your function will always return the same value, you can safely compute it once and always return that computed value for these specific arguments.

Let's look at the trivial implementation that is usually brought up for teaching purposes:

```
const memoize = yourFunction => {
  const cache = {};

  return (...args) => {
    const cacheKey = JSON.stringify(args);
    if (!cache[cacheKey]) {
        cache[cacheKey] = yourFunction(...args);
    }
    return cache[cacheKey];
  };
};
```

This is a powerful technique and is used in the reselect library.

Referential transparency

Pure functions are **referentially transparent**, meaning that their function invocation can be replaced with its corresponding outcome for a given argument.

Now, look at the examples of referentially-transparent and referentially-opaque functions:

```
let globalValue = 0;

const inc1 = (num) => { // Referentially opaque (has side effects)
```

```
    globalValue += 1;
    return num + globalValue;
  }

  const inc2 = (num) => { // Referentially transparent
    return num + 1;
  }
```

Let's imagine a mathematical expression:

```
inc(4) + inc(4) * 5

// With referentially transparent function you can simplify to:
inc(4) * ( 1 + 1*5 )
// and even to
inc(4) * 6
```

Be aware that you need to avoid such simplifications if your function is not referentially transparent. Expressions such as the preceding or x() + x() * 0 are tempting gotchas.

Whether you make any use of it or not is up to you. Also, see the *Further reading* section at the end of the chapter.

Everything but monads

The term monad has been infamous for many years. Not because it's an amazingly useful construct, but because of the complexity it introduces. There is also a common belief that once you understand monads, you lose the capability to explain them.

> *"In order to understand monads, you need to first learn Haskell and Category Theory. I think this is like saying: In order to understand burritos, you must first learn Spanish."*
>
> *- Douglas Crockford: Monads and Gonads (YUIConf Evening Keynote)*
> https://www.youtube.com/watch?v=dkZFtimgAcM.

A monad is a way of composing functions despite special circumstances, such as nullable values, side-effects, computations, or just conditional execution. Such a definition of a monad makes it a context holder. That's why the monad of X is not equivalent to X. This X Before being treated as monad<X>, this X something needs to be lifted first, which simply means creation of the required context. If we do not need monad<X> anymore, we can flatten the structure to just X, which is the equivalent of losing a context.

It's like unwrapping a present for Christmas. You are pretty sure there is a present in there, but it depends on whether you were nice throughout the year. In some rare cases of misbehavior, you may end up with the stick or lump of coal in there. This is how the Maybe<X> monad works. It may be X or nothing. It works great with nullable API values.

Call me Maybe

There is one place in our code that begs for simplification. Take a look at the taskSelector:

```
export const tasksSelector = state => state.tasks;

export const tasksEntitiesSelector = createSelector(
    tasksSelector,
    tasks => (tasks ? tasks.get('entities') : null)
);

export const getTaskById = taskId => createSelector(
    tasksEntitiesSelector,
    entities => (entities
        ? entities.find(task => task.id === taskId)
        : null)
);
```

We constantly fear whether we received something or null. This is a perfect case to delegate such work to the Maybe monad. Once we implement Maybe, the following code will be fully functional:

```
import Maybe from '../../../../utils/Maybe';

export const tasksSelector = state => Maybe(state).map(x => x.tasks);

export const tasksEntitiesSelector = createSelector(
    tasksSelector,
    maybeTasks => maybeTasks.map(tasks => tasks.get('entities'))
);

export const getTaskById = taskId => createSelector(
    tasksEntitiesSelector,
    entities => entities.map(e => e.find(task => task.id === taskId))
);
```

Okay, so far you know a little about the `Maybe` monad we need to implement: it needs to be nothing when `null/undefined` or `Something` when `null` nor `undefined`:

```
const Maybe = (value) => {
    const Nothing = {
        // Some trivial implementation
    };
    const Something = val => ({
        // Some trivial implementation
    });

    return (typeof value === 'undefined' || value === null)
        ? Nothing
        : Something(value);
};
```

So far, very easy. The problem is, we did not implement neither `Nothing` nor `Something`. Don't worry, it is dead simple, just like in my comment.

We need both of them to react to three functions:

- `isNothing`
- `val`
- `map`

The first two functions are trivial:

- `isNothing`: `Nothing` returns `true`, `Something` returns `false`
- `val`: `Nothing` returns `null`, `Something` returns its value

The last one is `map`, which for `Nothing` should do nothing (return itself) and for `Something` it should apply the function to the value:

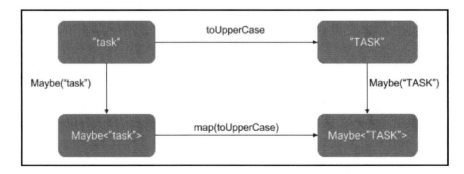

Applying toUpperCase on an ordinary string type and on the Maybe<string> monad using the map function

Let's implement this logic:

```
// src / Chapter 9 / Example 1 / src / utils / Maybe.js
const Maybe = (value) => {
    const Nothing = {
        map: () => this,
        isNothing: () => true,
        val: () => null
    };
    const Something = val => ({
        map: fn => Maybe(fn.call(this, val)),
        isNothing: () => false,
        val: () => val
    });

    return (typeof value === 'undefined' || value === null)
        ? Nothing
        : Something(value);
};

export default Maybe;
```

Here we go, it took us less than 20 lines. Our selectors are now using the `Maybe` monad. The last thing we need to do is fix the end usages; it should ask for the value after the selector call, as in the following example:

```
// src / Chapter 9 / Example 1
//          src/features/tasks/containers/TaskDetailsContainer.js

const mapStateToProps = (state, ownProps) => ({
    task: getTaskById(ownProps.taskId)(state).val()
});
```

Our `Maybe` implementation is a cool pattern to avoid the null-checking burden, but is it really a monad?

Monad interface requirements

More formally, the monad interface should define two basic operators:

- Return (a -> M a), an operation that takes the a type and wraps it into a monad (M a)
- Bind (M a -> (a -> M b) -> M b), an operation that takes two arguments: a monad of the a type, and a function that operates on a and returns the M b (a -> M b) monad

In these terms, our constructor function is the `return` function. However, our map function is not compliant with the `bind` requirements. It takes a function that turns a into b (a -> b), then our `map` function automatically wraps b into M b.

Beside this, our monad needs to obey three monad laws:

- Left identity:

```
// for all x, fn
Maybe(x).map(fn)  == Maybe(fn(x))
```

- Right identity:

```
// for all x
Maybe(x).map(x => x)  == Maybe(x)
```

- Associativity:

```
// for all x, fn, gn
Maybe(x).map(fn).map(gn)  == Maybe(x).map(x => gn(fn(x)));
```

Mathematical proof is outside the scope of this book. However, we can play with the laws and see whether they hold for some random examples:

```
// Left identity example
Maybe("randomtext")
.map(str => String.prototype.toUpperCase.call(str))
.val() // RANDOMTEXT

Maybe(String.prototype.toUpperCase.call("randomtext"))
.val()) // RANDOMTEXT

// Right identity example
Maybe("randomtext").map(str => str).val() // randomtext
Maybe("randomtext").val() // randomtext

// Associativity
const f = str => str.replace('1', 'one');
const g = str => str.slice(1);

Maybe("1 2 3").map(f).map(g).val() // ne 2 3
Maybe("1 2 3").map(str => g(f(str))).val() // ne 2 3
```

Higher-order functions

We have learned about higher-order components, and in this section, we will have a look at the more general concept, called higher-order functions.

Have a look at the example. It's pretty straightforward. You wouldn't even notice you created anything special:

```
const add5 = x => x + 5; // function
const applyTwice = (f, x) => f(f(x)); // higher order function


applyTwice(add5, 7); // 17
```

So what is a higher-order function?

A higher-order function is a function that does one of the following:

- Takes one or more functions as an argument
- Returns a function

That's it; it's so simple.

Examples of higher-order functions

There are a number of functions that are higher-order functions and you use them on a daily basis:

- `Array.prototype.map`:

```
someArray.map(function callback(currentValue, index, array){
    // Return new element
});

// or in the shorter form
someArray.map((currentValue, index, array) => { //... });
```

- `Array.prototype.filter`:

```
someArray.filter(function callback(currentValue, index, array){
    // Returns true or false
});

// or in the shorter form
someArray.filter((currentValue, index, array) => { //... });
```

- `Array.prototype.reduce`:

```
someArray.reduce(
    function callback(previousValue, currentValue, index, array){
        // Returns whatever
    },
    initialValue
);

// or in the shorter form
someArray.reduce((previousValue, currentValue, index, array) => {
    // ...
}, initialValue);

// previousValue is usually referred as accumulator or short acc
// reduce callback is also referred as fold function
```

And, of course, functions such as `compose`, `call`, or `curry`, which we have learned about already.

In general, any function that takes a callback is a higher-order function. You use such functions everywhere.

Do you remember how nicely those compose? See the following:

```
someArray
    .map(...)
    .filter(...)
    .map(...)
    .reduce(...)
```

But some of them don't, such as callbacks. Have you heard of callback hell?

A callback in a callback in a callback, this is a callback hell. That's why Promises were invented.

And then, all of a sudden, `Promise` hell started, so wise people created a syntactic sugar for promises: `async` and `await`.

Functional languages aside

To begin, please read this interesting opinion from David.

> "Wait, wait, wait. What does the performance of persistent data structures have to do with the future of JavaScript MVCs?
>
> A whole lot.
>
> We'll see how, perhaps unintuitively, immutable data allows a new library, Om, to outperform a reasonably performant JavaScript MVC like Backbone.js without hand optimization from the user. Om itself is built upon the absolutely wonderful React library from Facebook."

> \- The Future of JavaScript MVC Frameworks
> David Nolen (swannodette), 17 December 2013
> http://swannodette.github.io/2013/12/17/the-future-of-javascript-mvcs.

At the time of writing (September 2018), Backbone is already out of business. Even the popularity of Angular struggles to compete with React. React took the market insanely fast and once it finally changed it's license to MIT, it even accelerated.

The fun fact is that **requestAnimationFrame (rAF)** is not such a big deal as once believed.

> *"We do batching between different setState()s within one event handler (everything is flushed when you exit it). For many cases this works well enough and doesn't have pitfalls of using rAF for every update.*
>
> *We are also looking at asynchronous rendering by default. But rAF doesn't really help much if the rendered tree is large. Instead we want to split non-critical updates in chunks using rIC until they're ready to be flushed.*
>
> *(...) We use a concept of "expiration". Updates coming from interactive events get very short expiration time (must flush soon), network events get more time (can wait). Based on that we decide what to flush and what to time-slice."*

> *\- Dan Abramov tweets*
> https://twitter.com/jaffathecake/status/952861127528124417.

The lesson I want you to learn from these two quotations is: don't take things for granted, do not glorify one approach over another, and learn in which circumstances one is better than the other. Functional programming is similar; it would be foolish to just abandon this chapter as I once thought. I had this feeling: is it relevant to React Native programmers? Yes, it is. If it is popular enough to flood many public PRs in the community, you are certainly going to be exposed to these concepts and I want you to be prepared.

Terminology

Don't be scared by Functors, EndoFunctors, CoMonads, and CoRoutines—take what is useful from the theoretical abstractions. Let theoretical experts take care of them. Math geeks have always been ahead and usually this is a good thing, but don't get too crazy. Business is business. Deadlines cannot wait for you to prove the greatest law in category theory.

Focus on understanding the immediate benefits, such as the ones outlined in this book. If you ever find yourself in a team that is opposed to functional programming patterns, do not enforce them. After all, it is not as important in JavaScript as it is in Haskell.

> *"Using fancy words instead of simple, common ones makes things harder to understand. Your writing will be clearer if you stick with a small vocabulary."*
>
> *- Sophie Alpert tweet (Engineering manager of React at Facebook)*
> `https://twitter.com/sophiebits/status/1033450495069761536.`

Building abstractions

At the beginning of this chapter, we benchmarked immutable libraries and compared their performance. As with everything, I highly encourage you to spend some time before you commit to any library, pattern, or way of doing things.

Most libraries that adopt functional programming patterns do so for a real benefit. If you are unsure, leave it to someone else, and stick to your well-known imperative patterns. It turns out that simple code often gets better optimizations on the engine level.

React is not obsessed with pure functions

When you dive into the React ecosystem for the first time, you may get a bit of a surprise. There are a lot of examples that use pure functions and talk about time travelling, using Redux, and about one store to rule them all.

The truth is, neither React nor Redux use only pure functions. In fact, there are a lot of functions in both libraries that perform mutations in the outer scope:

```
// Redux library code
// redux/src/createStore.js

let currentReducer = reducer
let currentState = preloadedState
let currentListeners = []
let nextListeners = currentListeners
let isDispatching = false

// Check yourself:
https://github.com/reduxjs/redux/blob/
1448a7c565801029b67a84848582c6e61822f572/src/createStore.js
```

These variables are being modified by other functions.

Now, look at the React way of remembering what the library warned about:

```
let didWarnAboutMaps = false;

// (...)

if (__DEV__) {
  if (iteratorFn === children.entries) {
    warning(
      didWarnAboutMaps,
      'Using Maps as children is unsupported (...)'
    );
    didWarnAboutMaps = true;
  }
}

// Check yourself
https://github.com/facebook/react/blob/
f9358c51c8de93abe3cdd0f4720b489befad8c48/packages/react/src/ReactChildren.
js
```

This little mutation depends on the environment.

> If you maintain a library with such checks, current build tools, such as webpack, can remove this dead code when building a production-minified file. By dead code, I mean code paths (like the preceding `if` statement) that will never be accessed because of the environment (production).

When it comes to Facebook in general, they are not ashamed to show that their code base is tricky in some places:

```
var React;
if (__DEV__) {
  React = require('React-dev');
} else {
  React = require('React-prod');
}


// TODO(T18802204): codemod all remaining callers in www
React.createClass = require('create-react-class/factory'){
  React.Component,
  React.isValidElement,
  new React.Component().updater,
);
React.PropTypes = require('prop-types');
```

Facebook codebase screenshot, posted by Dan Abramov on Twitter

Summary

In this chapter, we took a deep dive into one of the most esoteric branches of JavaScript programming. We learned about monads, how to use them for the greater good, and how not to care about the laws of math if we really don't need to. Then, we got comfortable using vocabulary such as pure functions, mutable/immutable objects, and referential transparency.

We know that there is a caching pattern for pure functions if we need it. This great approach can be useful in many Flux apps. You now can work effectively with selectors and make them dead simple using the Maybe monad, which takes away the null-checking burden.

With all of this expertise, it is now time to learn the challenges of maintaining dependencies and large code bases. In the next chapter, you will face a major challenge of every big code base, and believe me, every major company struggles with this at some point—no matter how many programming patterns they use or how many libraries they depend on.

Further reading

- A mostly adequate guide to functional programming—a free book on functional programming in JavaScript:

  `https://github.com/MostlyAdequate/mostly-adequate-guide`.

- Examples of cache functions that you may want to use with the Reselect library:

  `https://github.com/reduxjs/reselect#q-the-default-memoization-function-is-no-good-can-i-use-a-different-one`.

- Information on referential transparency:

  `https://softwareengineering.stackexchange.com/questions/254304/what-is-referential-transparency`.

- Eric's Elliott mastering JavaScript interview series episode, Pure Functions:

  `https://medium.com/javascript-scene/master-the-javascript-interview-what-is-a-pure-function-d1c076bec976`.

- A historical post that predicted the future, *The future of JavaScript MVCs*:

  `http://swannodette.github.io/2013/12/17/the-future-of-javascript-mvcs`.

- This is old but still worth a read, *A General Theory of Reactivity*:

  `https://github.com/kriskowal/gtor`.

- The following book on FP in JavaScript, *JavaScript Allonge* (free to read online):

  ```
  https://leanpub.com/javascriptallongesix/read#leanpub-auto-about-
  javascript-allong.
  ```

- Monad laws (Haskell Wiki):

  ```
  https://wiki.haskell.org/Monad_laws.
  ```

- Douglas Crockford, Monads and Gonads:

  ```
  https://www.youtube.com/watch?v=dkZFtimgAcM.
  ```

- How Immutable.js is using the Trie graph to optimize writing operations:

  ```
  https://medium.com/@dtinth/immutable-js-persistent-data-structures-
  and-structural-sharing-6d163fbd73d2
  ```

  ```
  https://en.wikipedia.org/wiki/Trie.
  ```

- Should React use `requestAnimationFrame` by default:

  ```
  https://github.com/facebook/react/issues/11171.
  ```

- An awesome functional programming collection on GitHub:

  ```
  https://github.com/xgrommx/awesome-functional-programming/blob/master/
  README.md.
  ```

- If you fell in love with functional programming, here is a very good resource, Learn You a Haskell for Great Good (requires Haskell understanding):

  ```
  http://learnyouahaskell.com/chapters.
  ```

10
Managing Dependencies

This chapter is dedicated to managing dependencies, namely libraries, that your mobile applications rely on. Most current applications abuse the singleton pattern. However, I strongly believe that, one day, JavaScript developers will adopt well-known **dependency injection** (**DI**) patterns. Even if they decide to use the singleton pattern, it will be way easier to refactor. In this chapter, we will focus on the React context and how libraries such as Redux leverage the DI mechanism. This is the safest alternative to use if you really want to step up your code and make it easily testable. We will dive into the code in the React Redux library, which uses the React context extensively. You will also understand why the JavaScript world is so slow to abandon the singleton pattern.

In this chapter, you will learn about the following topics:

- The singleton pattern
- The DI pattern and its flavors in ECMAScript
- The storybook pattern, to increase productivity and document your components
- The React context API
- How to manage large code bases

Get ready, as we will start off with the singleton pattern straightaway.

The singleton pattern

The singleton pattern is a class that can have only one instance. By its design, whenever we attempt to create a new instance, it will either create an instance for the first time or return the one that was created previously.

How is this pattern useful? If we want to have a single manager for certain things, this comes in handy, whether it be an API manager or cache manager. For instance, if you need to authorize the API to get the token, you will only want to do this once. The first instance will initiate whatever work is necessary and then any other instance will reuse the work that has already been done. This use case was abused mostly by server-side applications, but more and more people have come to realize that there are better alternatives.

Such use cases can nowadays be easily countered by better patterns. Instead of creating a singleton pattern, you could simply store the token in a cache, and in any new instance, verify if the token is already in the cache. If it is, you can skip authorization and use the token. This trick uses the well-known fact that a cache is the one centralized place for storing data. In this context, it serves as a singleton store for us. Whether it be a cache for a client or cloud server, it's exactly the same thing, with the exception that on the server, it may be more costly to call.

Implementing the singleton pattern in ECMAScript

Although using the singleton pattern is discouraged nowadays, it is very beneficial to learn how to create this mechanism. For this code example, we will use ECMAScript 6 classes and ECMAScript 7 static fields:

```
export default class Singleton {
    static instance;

    constructor() {
        if (Singleton.instance) {
            return Singleton.instance;
        }

        this.instance = this;
    }
}
```

We are changing the behavior of the constructor. First, before returning anything, we need to check if the instance has already been created. If so, the current call returns that instance instead.

Why using the singleton pattern is discouraged

`Singleton` is sometimes treated as a `global` variable. If you attempt to import it from many different places and your use case is just sharing the same instance, you are probably abusing the pattern. This way, you tightly couple different pieces to the exact imported object. It is one of the vital signs of **code smell** if you use a `global` variable instead of passing it down.

On top of that, `Singleton` is very unpredictable in terms of testing. You receive something that is an effect of mutation. It may be a new object, or the object previously created. You may be tempted to use this to synchronize some form of a state. For instance, let's look at the following example:

```
export default class Singleton {
    static instance;

    constructor() {
        if (Singleton.instance) {
            return Singleton.instance;
        }

        this.name = 'DEFAULT_NAME';
        this.instance = this;
    }

    getName() {
        return this.name;
    }

    setName(name) {
        this.name = name;
    }
}
```

This makes `Singleton` not only globally shared, but also globally mutable. This is a horrible story if you want to make it predictable. It generally defeats everything we learned about in `Chapter 9`, *Elements of Functional Programming Patterns*.

You need to reassure every consumer component that it is ready to handle any type of data that comes from a singleton. This requires an exponential number of tests, and thus kills productivity. This is unacceptable.

Later on in this chapter, you will find a solution that will fix all of these issues via DI.

The many singleton flavors in JavaScript

To be honest, beyond just the previous implementation, we can see many other variations in order to achieve the same thing. Let's discuss them.

In the following code, the singleton has already been exported as an `instance`:

```
class Singleton {
    static instance;
    constructor() {
        if (Singleton.instance) {
            return Singleton.instance;
        }

        this.instance = this;
    }
}

export default new Singleton();
```

This looks like a good improvement unless your `Singleton` requires arguments. If so, the `Singleton` is exported in such a way that it is also harder to test and may only accept hard-coded dependencies.

Sometimes, your `Singleton` may be very small and only an object will be enough:

```
export default {
    apiRoot: API_URL,
    fetchData() {
        // ...
    },
};
```

Refactoring this pattern we may lead to a well-known syntax for any mature JavaScript developer:

```
// ./apiSingleton.js
export const apiRoot = API_URL;
export const fetchData = () => {
    // ...
```

```
}

// Then import as shown below
import * as API from './apiSingleton'
```

The last example may start worrying you, and you may have started asking yourself—am I unknowingly using singletons? I bet you are. But this is not the end of the world, as long as you inject them properly. Let's go through a section on ECMAScript and JavaScript module approaches. This is important knowledge for any JavaScript programmer.

 Be careful, as some module bundlers do not guarantee that modules will be instantiated only once. Tools such as webpack may internally, for the sake of optimization or compatibility, instantiate some modules multiple times.

ES6 modules and beyond

One of the best aspects of ES6 modules is the static nature of import and export declarations. Thanks to this, we can check at compile time if imports and exports are correct, perform injections (such as polyfills for older browsers), and bundle them together if necessary (like webpack does). These are amazing positives that save us a lot of runtime checking that would possibly slow our application down.

However, some people abuse how ES6 modules work. The syntax is super easy—you can import module wherever and use it easily. This is a gotcha. You may not want to abuse importing.

The DI pattern

Importing and using an imported value in the same file locks that file to the concrete implementation. For instance, check out the following app code implementation:

```
import AddTaskContainer from '../path/to/AddTaskContainer';
import TaskListContainer from '../path/to/TaskListContainer';

export const TasksSection = () => (
    <View>
        <AddTaskContainer />
        <TaskListContainer />
    </View>
);
```

In this code example, the `TasksSection` component is composed of two container components, `AddTaskContainer` and `TaskListContainer`. The important fact is that you cannot modify either of the container components if you are a consumer of the `TasksSection` component. You need to rely on the implementations provided by imported modules.

To fix this problem, we can use the DI pattern. We are essentially passing dependencies to the component as props. In this example, this would look as follows:

```
export const TasksSection = ({
    AddTaskContainer,
    TaskListContainer
}) => (
    <View>
        <AddTaskContainer />
        <TaskListContainer />
    </View>
);
```

If somebody is not interested in passing these components, we can create a container that will provide them. However, in cases where we want to substitute containers for something else, this comes in very handy, for instance, in tests or in storybooks! What is storybook? Keep reading.

Using the DI pattern with storybooks

A storybook is a way to document your components. As your application grows, you may quickly end up with hundreds of components. If you build a serious application, most of them are aligned to a design specification and all of the expected features will have been implemented. The trick is knowing which props to send to achieve the expected result. Storybook makes this simple. When you implement a component, you also create a storybook for different scenarios. Check out the following trivial example for the `Button` component:

Example storybook of the Button component

By selecting scenarios in the left panel, you can quickly look up how components look with different props.

I have installed Storybook for you to play with in `src/Example 10/Exercise 1`. You can launch Storybook by running either `yarn run ios:storybook` or `yarn run android:storybook` from that directory.

> If you would like to learn how to set up Storybook yourself, check out the official documentation at
> `https://github.com/storybooks/storybook/tree/master/app/react-native`.
> Most of the configuration files you will need to add should go in the `storybook` directory within the project.

The installation command-line interface that storybook provides sets up playground stories for you. Those are the ones in the preceding screenshot (the `Button` with text and with emojis).

Time to add our own stories. Let's start with something easy – the `TaskList` component. This component is ideal for storybooking because it is very well-developed. It handles errors, and displays various messages depending on the loading state or error state. It can display 0 tasks, 1 task, and 2 or more tasks. There are a lot of stories to look at:

```
// src/Chapter_10/Example_1/src/features/tasks/stories/story.js

storiesOf('TaskList', module)
    .addDecorator(getStory => (
        <ScrollView
style={generalStyles.content}>{getStory()}</ScrollView>
    ))
    .add('with one task', () => (
        <TaskList
            tasks={Immutable.List([exampleData.tasks[0]])}
            hasError={false}
            isLoading={false}
        />
    ))
    .add('with 7 tasks', () => (
        <TaskList
            tasks={Immutable.List(exampleData.tasks)}
            hasError={false}
            isLoading={false}
        />
    ));
```

In the preceding code example, we created our first story for the `TaskList` component. The `storiesOf` function comes with storybook. Then, in a decorator, we wrapped every story with a scrollable view and general styles that apply padding to the left and right. In the end, we created two stories using the `add` function: `TaskList` with only one story and `TaskList` with 7 stories.

Unfortunately, our code breaks with the following error:

> **Invariant Violation: withNavigation can only be used on a view hierarchy of a navigator. The wrapped component is unable to get access to navigation from props or context.**
> **– Runtime error in application**

The problem lies in the `NavButton` component that we have implemented. It uses the `withNavigation` HOC, which effectively requires context already:

```
// src/ Chapter_10/ Example_1/ src/ components/ NavigateButton.js

export default withNavigation(NavigateButton);
```

Fortunately, `withNavigation` is already using the DI pattern thanks to relying on the React context. What we need to do is inject the required context (navigation) into our storybook example. To do so, we need to use `NavigationProvider` from react-navigation:

```
// src/ Chapter_10/ Example_1/ src/ features/ tasks/ stories/ story.js
storiesOf('TaskList', module)
    .addDecorator(getStory => (
        <NavigationProvider
            value={{
                navigate: action('navigate')
            }}
        >
            <ScrollView
style={generalStyles.content}>{getStory()}</ScrollView>
        </NavigationProvider>
    ))
    .add('with one task', () => (
        // ...
    ))
    .add('with 7 tasks', () => (
        // ...
    ));
```

Finally, we can admire our two newly created stories:

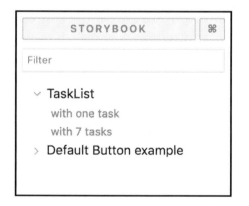

TaskList component stories in storybook

When you select one of them, it will be displayed on the simulator:

TaskList stories displayed on the iPhone X simulators

With a little more effort, we can add further stories to this storybook. For instance, let's try loading an error case:

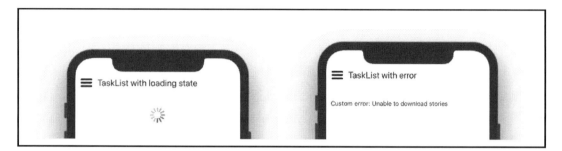

TaskList stories for loading state and error state

We can also create a story for a combination such as the one shown in the preceding screenshot:

TaskList story with error and loading state

Nested stories with DI

The preceding example is good enough. It creates a storybook, it is reusable, and everyone is happy. However, as the application grows and we add more stories, it is not always possible to fix this with a `Provider`, or the `Provider` may have been used in too many stories.

In this section, we will refactor our code to be able to inject our own component instead of importing the NavButton container. As our goal is to retain the functionality that we had previously, in the storybook we will inject a NavButton story, which will take care of the navigation problem. However, in the normal app, we will inject the NavButton container just as before but into the TaskList container. The win here is the fact that we will not need to use NavigationProvider at all:

```
// src/Chapter_10/Example_1/src/features/tasks/views/TaskList.js

const TaskList = ({
    tasks, isLoading, hasError, errorMsg, NavButton
}) => (
    <View style={styles.taskList}>
        // ...
                <View style={styles.taskActions}>
                    <NavButton
                        data={{ taskId: task.id }}
                        to="Task"
                        text="Details"
                    />
                </View>
        // ...
    </View>
);
```

From now on, TaskList expects the NavButton component in props. We need to comply with these prop expectations, both in the container and in the storybook. The following is the code for the first container:

```
// src/Chapter_10/Example_1/src/features/tasks/containers/TaskList.js
import NavButton from '../../../components/NavigateButton';

const mapStateToProps = state => ({
    // ...
    NavButton
});

const TasksContainer = connect(mapStateToProps)(fetchTasks(TaskListView));
```

Time for the fun part. We need to solve a storybook problem. To accomplish our goal with DI, we will create a separate storybook for NavButton. To fix the TaskList storybook, we will import the NavButton story and inject it as a NavButton component to the TaskList view.

This may sound complicated, but let's see this in the following example.

To create the NavButton story, we need to refactor NavButton into a view and a container:

```
// src/Chapter_10/Example_1/src/components/NavigateButton/index.js

// container for NavButtonView

import { withNavigation } from 'react-navigation';
import NavButtonView from './view';

export default withNavigation(NavButtonView);
```

The view is just the same as before—I have moved the code to view.js in the NavigateButton directory, next to the preceding container. We can now proceed with the creation of the storybook:

```
// src/Chapter_10/Example_1/src/components/NavigateButton/story.js

import {
    withBackText,
    withDetailsText,
    withEmojisText
} from './examples';
// ...

storiesOf('NavButton', module)
    .addDecorator(scrollViewDecorator)
    .add('with details text', withDetailsText)
    .add('with back text', withBackText)
    .add('with emojis text', withEmojisText);

// src/Chapter_10/Example_1/src/components/NavigateButton/examples.js
// ...
export const withDetailsText = () => (
    <NavButton
        navigation={{ navigate: () => action('navigate') }}
        text="Details"
        to=""
        data={{}}
    />
);
```

In this code example, I have introduced a little improvement. Separation of concerns examples go into separate files so that they can be reused in areas other than just storybooks, for instance, in snapshot tests.

Mocking `navigation` is now very simple and straightforward. We just substitute the `navigation` object and the `navigate` function inside it.

We are now ready to inject that example as the `NavButton` component in the `TaskList` story:

```
// src/Chapter_10/Example_2/src/features/tasks/stories/story.js

import NavButtonExample from '../../../components/NavigateButton/examples';

storiesOf('TaskList', module)
    .addDecorator(scrollViewDecorator)
    .add('with one task', () => (
        <TaskList
            tasks={Immutable.List([exampleData.tasks[0]])}
            hasError={false}
            isLoading={false}
            NavButton={NavButtonExample}
        />
    ))
    // ... rest of the TaskList stories
```

At the same time, our `scrollViewDecorator` is minimal:

```
// src/ Chapter_10/ Example_2/ src/ utils/ scrollViewDecorator.js

const scrollViewDecorator = getStory => (
    <ScrollView style={generalStyles.content}>{getStory()}</ScrollView>
);
```

DI with React context

In the previous section, we used DI in a very straightforward way by just injecting components. React comes with its own mechanism for DI.

React context can be used to inject dependencies into components that are very far in the chain from the container component. This makes React context a great fit for global dependencies that are reused across the whole application.

Good examples of such a global dependency are a theme configuration, a logger, a dispatcher, a logged in user object, or language options.

Using the React Context API

To learn about the React Context API, we will use a simple language selector. I have created a component that allows us to select one of two languages, either English or Polish. It stores the selected language in the Redux store:

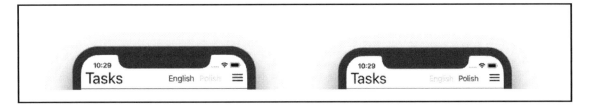

Language selector in the application's header and the left image shows English selected; the right image shows Polish selected

Our goal is now to expose language through the React context API. To do so, we need to use the `createContext` function that was imported from React. This function will return an object containing the `Provider` and `Consumer` components:

```
// src/ Chapter_10/ Example_3/ src/ features/ language/ context.js
import { createContext } from 'react';
import { LANG_ENGLISH } from './constants';

// First function argument represents default value
const { Provider, Consumer } = createContext(LANG_ENGLISH);

export const LanguageProvider = Provider;
export const LanguageConsumer = Consumer;
```

`LanguageConsumer` is used to get a value that traverses the component tree. The first `LanguageProvider` it encounters will provide the value; otherwise, if there is no `LanguageProvider`, the default value from the `createContext` call will be used.

To ensure that every component has access to language, we should add
`LanguageProvider` in the root, preferably in the screens component. To easily do so using
already learned patterns, I have created a higher-order component called
`withLanguageProvider`:

```
src/Chapter_10/Example_3/src/features/language/hocs/withLanguageProvider.js
```

```
const withLanguageProvider = WrappedComponent => connect(state => ({
    language: languageSelector(state)
}))(({ language, ...otherProps }) => (
    <LanguageProvider value={language}>
        <WrappedComponent {...otherProps} />
    </LanguageProvider>
));

export default withLanguageProvider;
```

We can use this utility to wrap the screen component in the following way:

```
withStoreProvider(withLanguageProvider(createDrawerNavigator({
    Home: TabNavigation,
    Profile: ProfileScreen,
    Settings: SettingsScreen
})));
```

Please notice the refactoring – we also provide the store in the same way.

Having language in the context, we can proceed with the consumption in any lower level
components, for instance, in the `TaskList` component:

```
// src/Chapter_10/Example_3/src/features/tasks/views/TaskList.js
// ...

<LanguageConsumer>
    {language => (
        <Text style={styles.selectedLanguage}>
            Selected language: {language}
        </Text>
    )}
</LanguageConsumer>
```

The result is shown in following screenshot:

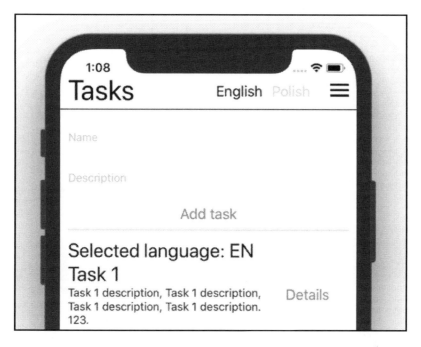

Example usage of LanguageConsumer in the TaskList component

Please note that this is only an example in order to learn about the context API. No actual translation is being performed. To add translations to your app, use the React Intl library from Yahoo!. It also exposes `Provider` for your convenience (https://github.com/yahoo/react-intl).

React Redux aside

If you paid close attention to the previous examples, you may have spotted an interesting part – `withStoreProvider`. This is a higher order component I made to wrap the root component with the `react-redux` store `Provider`:

```
import { Provider } from 'react-redux';
// ...
<Provider store={store}>
    <WrappedComponent {...props} />
</Provider>
```

The `Provider` that is exposed is very similar to the React context API. The context was in the React library for a long time, along with an experimental API. However, the newest context API was introduced with React 16 and you may notice that old libraries still use their own custom providers. For instance, have a look at the react-redux `Provider` implementation, as follows:

```
class Provider extends Component {
    getChildContext() {
        return { [storeKey]: this[storeKey], [subscriptionKey]: null }
    }

    constructor(props, context) {
        super(props, context)
        this[storeKey] = props.store;
    }

    render() {
        return Children.only(this.props.children)
    }
}

// Full implementation available in react-redux source files
//
https://github.com/reduxjs/react-redux/blob/73691e5a8d016ef9490bb20feae8671
f3b8f32eb/src/components/Provider.js
```

This is how the react-redux `connect` function has access to your Redux store. Instead of the `Consumer` API, there is the `connect` function, which we use instead to access the store. You are probably already used to it. Treat this as a guideline on how to use exposed providers or consumers.

Managing the code base

Our code base has started growing. We have taken the first steps in addressing the monolithic architecture problem and we have a pretty good file structure so far:

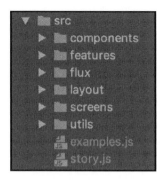

Current src/ directory structure

Although good enough for now, we should rethink our approach and create rules if we want to make this project bigger.

Quick wins

When a new developer joins the project, it may be a little challenging for them to understand our code base. Let's address a few easy fixes.

To start with, where is the entry file for our application? It's in the root directory. However, there is no clear entry point in the source (src/) directory. This is okay, but it would be handy to have it close to the story and examples. At a glance, you will have examples, the storybook, and the app root to lookup.

In addition, we can refactor the current ScreenRoot component. It serves as AppRoot and is wrapped in two HOCs. As you already know, such coupling is not a good thing. I have made a little refactor. Have a look at the new structure:

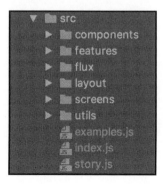

The entry point to the application is now clearly visible (index.js)

We have achieved a very quick win; it is now way easier to find the root component. Now, let's look at the `components` and `features` directories:

Components and features directories

The components folder was initially meant to collect stateless components. As the application grew, we quickly realized that having a shared directory for just stateless components is not enough. We want to reuse stateful ones too. Thus, we should rename the `components` directory to `common`. It better represents what the directory is:

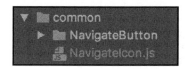

The Components directory has been renamed to common

Another issue that we will quickly notice is the fact that the language directory under features only creates confusion. It's primarily `LanguageSwitcher`, not the `language` in general. We have put this under features only because we want to consume the language in the app feature components. Is language context a feature? Not really; it is some sort of feature, but not in the context of user experience. This creates confusion.

We should do two things:

1. Move the context to the common directory as we plan to reuse `LanguageConsumer` in the whole app.
2. Admit that we will not reuse the `LanguageSwitcher` component and place it within the layout directory as it is not meant to be used anywhere beyond layout components.

Once we do this, our app structure is again cleaner:

Language directory has been split into LanguageSwitcher and LanguageContext

`LanguageContext` is now easy to find. Similarly, we do not need to bother about the `LanguageSwitcher` implementation until we change the layout.

The util directory creates a similar confusion, just like the initial language directory does. We can safely move it to the `common` directory:

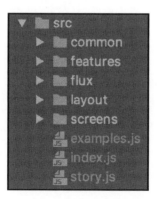

The refactored directory structure

Now, any new developer joining the project can quickly get a clear idea of it. `screens`, `layout`, `flux`, `features`, and `common` are all very self-explanatory names.

Establishing conventions

Whenever you build a big project, relying on the developer's own judgement, like in the previous section, may not be enough. The inconsistency of approaches taken by different tech leads may quickly escalate and lead to tens of development hours being lost on exploring a code jungle.

If this sounds to you like a foreign problem, I can promise that in code bases with hundreds of developers working simultaneously every day, it is a very important pattern to establish clear guidelines and conventions.

Let's have a look at a few examples:

- **Linter**: Takes care of the code appearance guidelines and enforces them automatically. It may also enforce certain usage patterns and favor certain options over others if there is a list of alternatives.
- **Flux architecture**: The general architecture of how to connect and structure JavaScript code to solve common usage patterns. Not enforced automatically.
- **Pure reducers**: Reducers need to be as pure as an architectural decision of the Redux library. This is not enforced in the classic Flux architecture. This may or may not be enforced automatically.
- **Styles defined in JavaScript**: A solution that comes out of the box with React Native.

The list goes on. I hope it is enough to convince you that establishing conventions is a good thing. It does limit the available capabilities a little, but enables you to ship customer value much faster. React Native on its own is a good example that connects many different ecosystems to provide a unified way of developing mobile applications. It has proven to increase mobile developer's productivity significantly.

All big software companies approach similar convention problems. Some of them are so common that companies invest money into making them open source to make a name for themselves. Thanks to this, we have the following:

- React and React Native from Facebook
- TypeScript, a typed language on top of ECMAScript from Microsoft
- eslint configuration from Airbnb
- Internationalization library for React from Yahoo!
- Documentation on JavaScript from Mozilla
- Material design guidelines from Google, and many many more

This is changing the software world for the better.

I hope that you will apply this wisdom to your future projects. Please use it to enhance the productivity of your team and organization. If it is overkill right now, it is also a good sign that you have spotted that.

Summary

This chapter has addressed the common problems of dependencies in your application. As you strive to deliver bulletproof applications, you will find these patterns useful in tests. On top of that, you have also learned what a storybook is, that is, something that documents use cases for your components. You now can easily compose components and storybooks.

Ecosystem also embraces these patterns, and we have used the React Context API to pass language context down the component chain. You also had a glimpse into the react-redux implementation of `Provider`.

Brace yourself for the last chapter, which introduces types into your applications. We will finally ensure that passed variables match consumer function expectations. This will enable us to type everything in the application, instead of using just `PropTypes` for React views.

Further reading

- Directory structure guide by Atlaskit developers:
  This guideline will teach you about how a big code base can be maintained. It is one of the many examples on how to approach the scalability of frontend code bases which are maintained by multiple developers every day
  (`https://atlaskit.atlassian.com/docs/guides/directory-structure`).

- How Airbnb Is Using React Native:
  Tech talk about the Airbnb techstack, which needs to ship to three different platforms: the browser, Android, and iOS. Learn about the challenges that developers at Airbnb have faced
  (`https://www.youtube.com/watch?v=8qCociUB6aQ`).

- Rafael de Oleza - Building JavaScript bundles for React Native:
  Rafael explains how metro bundler in React Native works.
  (`https://www.youtube.com/watch?v=tX2lg59Wm7g`).

11
Type Checking Patterns

To be able to leave your application working and forget about any troubles, you need a way to make sure that all parts of your application match each other. Languages built on top of JavaScript or ECMAScript, such as Flow or TypeScript, bring type systems to your application. Thanks to these, you will know that no one is sending the wrong data to your functions or components. We have already used `PropTypes` for assertions in components. Now we will apply this concept to any JavaScript variable.

In this chapter, you will learn about the following:

- The basics of type systems
- How to assign types to functions and variables
- What contract tests are; for instance, the Pact test
- Generics and union types
- Tips on how to solve type problems
- How type systems use nominal and structural typing

Introduction to types

In ECMAScript, we have seven implicit types. Six of them are primitives.

The six data types that are primitives are as follows:

- Boolean.
- Number.
- String.
- Null.
- Undefined.
- Symbol—a unique identifier introduced in ECMAScript. Its purpose is to guarantee uniqueness. This is used commonly as a unique key in objects.

The seventh type is objects.

Functions and arrays are also objects. Generally, anything that is not a primitive type is an object.

Whenever you assign a value to a variable, the type is automatically determined. Based on the type, there are some rules that apply.

Primitive function arguments are passed by value. Objects are passed by reference.

Every variable is stored in memory in the form of zeros and ones. Passing by value means that the called function parameter will be copied. This means the creation of a new object that has a new reference. Passing by reference means passing just the reference to the object—if somebody makes changes to the referenced memory, then it will affect everyone who uses this reference.

Let's look at the examples of the mechanism of passing by value:

```
// Passing by value

function increase(x) {
    x = x + 1;
    return x;
}

var num = 5;
increase(num);
console.log(num); // prints 5
```

The num variable has not been changed because, on function call, the value was copied. The x variable referenced a completely new variable in the memory. Let's now look at a similar example, but with an object:

```
// Passing by reference

function increase(obj) {
    obj.x = obj.x + 1;
    return obj;
}

var numObj = { x: 5 };
increase(numObj);
console.log(numObj); // prints { x: 6 }
```

This time, we passed the `numObj` object to the function. It has been passed by reference, and so was not copied. When we changed the `obj` variable, it affected `numObj` externally.

However, when we invoke the preceding functions, we do not check the types. By default, we can pass anything. If our function cannot handle the passed variable, then it will break with some kind of error.

Let's have a look at the hidden and unexpected behavior that may occur with usage of the `increase` function:

```
function increase(obj) {
    obj.x = obj.x + 1;
    return obj;
}

var numObj = { x: "5" };
increase(numObj);
console.log(numObj); // prints { x: "51" }
```

The `increase` function computes `51` when we add `"5"` and `1`. This is how JavaScript works—it does implicit type conversion to be able to perform an operation.

Do we have a way to prevent this and save developers from accidental mistakes? Yes, we can do a runtime check to reassess that the variable is of a certain type:

```
// Runtime checking if obj.x is a number

function increase(obj) {
    if (typeof obj.x === 'number') {
        obj.x = obj.x + 1;
        return obj;
    } else {
        throw new Error("Obj.x must be a number");
    }
}

var numObj = { x: "5" };
increase(numObj);
console.log(numObj); // do not print, an Error message is shown
// Uncaught Error: Obj.x must be a number
```

A runtime check is a check that is performed while the code is evaluated. It is part of the code execution phase and affects the application speed. We will look more closely at runtime checking later on in this chapter, in the section on solving problems in runtime validation.

When the `Error` message is thrown, we also need to use error boundaries for component replacement or some `try{}catch(){}` syntax for handling async code errors.

 If you did not read this book from the beginning, then you may find it handy to go back to `Chapter 2`, *View Patterns*, to learn more about error boundaries in React.

However, we did not check if the `obj` variable is of the `Object` type! Such runtime checks can be added, but let's look at something much more convenient—TypeScript, the type checking language built on top of JavaScript.

Introduction to TypeScript

TypeScript brings types to our code. We can explicitly express the requirement that a function accepts only a specific variable type. Let's look at how we could use the example from the previous section with types from TypeScript:

```
type ObjXType = {
    x: number
}

function increase(obj: ObjXType) {
    obj.x = obj.x + 1;
    return obj;
}

var numObj = { x: "5" };
increase(numObj);
console.log(numObj);
```

This code will not compile. The static check will exit with an error saying that the code base is corrupted because types do not match.

The following error will be shown:

```
Argument of type '{ x: string; }' is not assignable to parameter of type
'ObjXType'.
  Types of property 'x' are incompatible.
  Type 'string' is not assignable to type 'number'.
```

TypeScript has caught us red-handed. We need to fix the error. Such code will never reach the end user until the developer fixes the error.

Configuring TypeScript

For your convenience, I have configured TypeScript in our repository. You can check it under `src/Chapter 11/Example 1` in the code files.

There are a few things I want you to understand.

TypeScript comes with its own configuration file, called `tsconfig.json`. In this file, you will find multiple configuration properties that control how strict the TypeScript compiler is. You can find a detailed list of the properties and explanations in the official documentation at `https://www.typescriptlang.org/docs/handbook/compiler-options.html`.

Among the options, you can find `outDir`. This specifies where the compiler output should be saved. In our repository, it is set to `"outDir": "build/dist"`. Our application, from now on, will run the compiled code from the `build/dist` directory. Hence, I have changed the root `App.js` file as follows:

```
// src/ Chapter_11/ Example_1_TypeScript_support/ App.js

import StandaloneApp from './build/dist/Root';
import StoryBookApp from './build/dist/storybook';

// ...
export default process.env['REACT_NATIVE_IS_STORY_BOOK'] ? StoryBookApp :
StandaloneApp;
```

Now that you understand the configuration changes, we can now proceed with learning basic typing.

Learning the basic types

To get the most out of TypeScript, you should type as much code as possible. However, our application did not have types before. In the case of a large application, you obviously cannot suddenly add types everywhere. Hence, we will gradually increase application type coverage.

TypeScript's list of basic types is quite long—Boolean, number, string, array, tuple, enum, any, void, null, undefined, never, and object. If you are unfamiliar with any of the them, then kindly please check the following page:
`https://www.typescriptlang.org/docs/handbook/basic-types.html`.

To start, let's look at one of the components that we used:

```
import PropTypes from 'prop-types';

export const NavigateButton = ({
    navigation, to, data, text
}) => (
    // ...
);

NavigateButton.propTypes = {
    // ...
};
```

We will now switch to TypeScript. Let's start with the `Prop` types:

```
import {
    NavigationParams, NavigationScreenProp, NavigationState
} from 'react-navigation';

type NavigateButtonProps = {
    to: string,
    data: any,
    text: string,
    navigation: NavigationScreenProp<NavigationState, NavigationParams>
};
```

In these little examples, we have defined the structure of the `NavigationButton` props. The `data` prop is of the `any` type, as we do not control what kind of data is being passed.

The `navigation` prop uses types defined by the `react-navigation` library. This is crucial to reuse already exposed types. In the project files, I have installed the `react-navigation` types using the `yarn add @types/react-navigation` command.

We can proceed with adding types to `NavigationButton`:

```
export const NavigateButton:React.SFC<NavigateButtonProps> = ({
    navigation, to, data, text
}) => (
    // ...
);

// Full example available at
// src/ Chapter_11/ Example_1/ src/ common/ NavigateButton/ view.tsx
```

SFC type is exported by React library. It is a generic type that can accept any possible prop types definition. Hence, we need to specify what kind of prop type it is: SFC<NavigateButtonProps>.

That's it—we also need to remove the old NavigateButton.propTypes definition at the bottom. From now on, TypeScript will validate the types passed on the NavigateButton function.

enums and constants patterns

There is a concept that is long praised in any code base I have seen: constants. They save so much value that almost everybody agrees that it is a must to define variables that hold a specific constant value. If, instead, we copied it to every single place where we need them, it would be much harder to update the value.

Some constants need to be flexible, hence, wise developers extract them to configuration files. Such files are stored in the code base, and sometimes in many different flavors (for instance, for test: dev, quality assurance, and production environments).

In many cases, the constants we define allow only a constant set of valid values. For instance, if we were to define available environments, then we could create a list:

```
const ENV_TEST = 'environment_test';
// ...

const availableEnvironments = [ENV_TEST, ENV_DEV, ENV_QA, ENV_PROD]
```

In old-school programming in JavaScript, you would simply switch-case the environments and propagate relevant information to the specific objects in your application. If the environment was unrecognized, then if would fall into a default clause where it usually simply throws an error saying "unrecognized environment" and closes the application.

If you assume that, in TypeScript, you would not need to check such things, you are wrong. Whatever you consume from the outside needs runtime validation. You cannot allow JavaScript to fail on its own and blow up the application in an unpredictable manner. This is a huge "gotcha" that is often overlooked.

One of the most common problems you may run into is API change. If you expect the `http://XYZ` endpoint to return JSON with the `tasks` key, and you do not validate what was really returned to you, you are in trouble. For instance, if a separate team decides to change the key to `projectTasks`, and is not aware of your dependency on `tasks`, it will surely lead to problems. How can we fix this?

The expected return values on your APIs is quite easy to enforce. A long time ago, the term contract tests was developed. This means creating a contract in both frontend and backend systems. Contracts cannot be changed without reassuring both code bases are ready. This is usually enforced by some automation tool, one of which may be Pact tests.

> "**Pact** (noun):
>
> A formal agreement between individuals or parties. "The country negotiated a trade pact with the US.
>
> Synonyms: agreement, protocol, deal, contract"
>
> `-Oxford Dictionaries`
> `(https://en.oxforddictionaries.com/definition/pact).`

If you look for a way to enforce this programmatically, have a look at `https://github.com/pact-foundation/pact-js`. This topic is tough and also requires knowledge of backend languages, hence it is out of this book's scope.

Once we are 100% sure that outside world data is validated, we may want to ensure that our own computations never lead to changing the variables (for instance, through immutability, see Chapter 9, *Elements of Functional Programming Patterns*) or if the change is expected, that it will always retain a value of the allowed set.

This is when TypeScript comes in handy. You can ensure that your computations will always lead to the one of the allowed states. You will not need any runtime validation. TypeScript will save you from unnecessary checks that, in large amounts, could result in slowing your app by a few miliseconds. Let's see how we can do this:

```
// src/ Chapter_11/
// Example_2/ src/ features/ tasks/ actions/ TasksActionTypes.ts

enum TasksActionType {
    ADD_TASK = 'ADD_TASK',
    TASKS_FETCH_START = 'TASKS_FETCH_START',
    TASKS_FETCH_COMPLETE = 'TASKS_FETCH_COMPLETE',
    TASKS_FETCH_ERROR = 'TASKS_FETCH_ERROR',
    TASK_FETCH_START = 'TASK_FETCH_START',
```

```
    TASK_FETCH_COMPLETE = 'TASK_FETCH_COMPLETE',
    TASK_FETCH_ERROR = 'TASK_FETCH_ERROR'
}
```

We have defined an `enum` type. If the variable is expected to be of the `TasksActionType` type, it can only be assigned the values from the preceding `enum TasksActionType`.

We can now define `AddTaskActionType`:

```
export type TaskAddFormData = {
    name: string,
    description: string
}

export type AddTaskActionType = {
    type: TasksActionType.ADD_TASK,
    task: TaskAddFormData
};
```

It will be used in the `addTask` action creator:

```
// src/ Chapter_11/
// Example_2/ src/ features/ tasks/ actions/ TaskActions.ts

const addTask = (task:TaskAddFormData): AddTaskActionType => ({
    type: TasksActionType.ADD_TASK,
    task
});
```

Now our action creator is type checked very well. If any developer, by mistake, changes the `type` object key to any other, for instance, `TasksActionType.TASK_FETCH_COMPLETE`, then TypeScript will detect that and show an incompatibility error.

We have `AddTaskActionType`, but how can we combine this with other action types that our reducer may accept? We can use union types.

Creating union types and intersections

A union type describes a value that can be one of several types. This is a great fit for our `Tasks` reducer type:

```
export type TaskReduxActionType =
    AddTaskActionType |
    TasksFetchActionType |
    TasksFetchCompleteActionType |
    TasksFetchErrorActionType |
```

```
    TaskFetchActionType |
    TaskFetchCompleteActionType |
    TaskFetchErrorActionType;
```

The union type is created with the | operator. It works just as if it was | was or. One type or another.

We can now use the previous type in the Reducer function:

```
// src/ Chapter_11/
// Example_3/ src/ features/ tasks/ state/ reducers/ tasksReducer.ts

const tasksReducer = (
    state = Immutable.Map<string, any>({
        entities: Immutable.List<TaskType>([]),
        isLoading: false,
        hasError: false,
        errorMsg: ''
    }),
    action:TaskReduxActionType
) => {
    // ...
}
```

To make TypeScript happy, we need to add types to all of the parameters. Hence, I have added the rest of the types. One of them is still missing: TaskType.

 In the preceding code example, you may be surprised by the Immutable.List<TaskType> notation, and especially the < > signs. Those need to be used because List is a generic type. We will talk about generic types in the next section.

To create TaskType, we could just write its type as follows:

```
type TaskType = {
    name: string,
    description: string
    likes: number,
    id: number
}
```

However, this is not reusing the type we have already created: TaskAddFormData. Whether you want to do so is a topic for another discussion. Let's assume we want to.

To reuse existing type and declare or create `TaskType` in the desired shape, we will need to use an intersection:

```
export type TaskAddFormData = {
    name: string,
    description: string
}

export type TaskType = TaskAddFormData & {
    likes: number,
    id: number
}
```

In this example, we used the & intersection operator to create a new type. The created type is an intersection of the types from the left-hand side and right-hand side of the & operator:

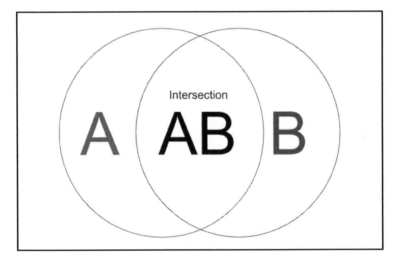

An intersection diagram, where the intersection is the space that is both in circle A and in circle B

An intersection of **A** and **B** possesses both the properties of **A** and **B**. Hence, the type that is created by an intersection of type **A** and type **B** must have both type **A** types and type **B** types. To summarize, `TaskType` must now be of the following shape:

```
{
    name: string,
    description: string
    likes: number,
    id: number
}
```

As you can see, intersections may be handy. Sometimes, when we rely on external libraries, we don't want to hardcode the key types as in the previous examples. Let's look at it again:

```
type NavigateButtonProps = {
    to: string,
    data: any,
    text: string,
    navigation: NavigationScreenProp<NavigationState, NavigationParams>
};
```

The navigation key is hardcoded in our type. We could have used an intersection to comply with possible future changes of the external library shape:

```
// src/ Chapter_11/
// Example_3/ src/ common/ NavigateButton/ view.tsx

import { NavigationInjectedProps, NavigationParams } from 'react-
navigation';

type NavigateButtonProps = {
    to: string,
    data: any,
    text: string,
} & NavigationInjectedProps<NavigationParams>;
```

In this example, we use the <> signs again. These are needed because `NavigationInjectedProps` is a generic type. Let's learn what generic types are.

Generic types

Generics allow you to write code that will handle any type of object. For instance, you know that a list is a generic type. You can make a list of anything. Hence, when we used `Immutable.List`, we had to specify what kind of objects the list will consist of:

```
Immutable.List<TaskType>
```

List of tasks. Let's now create our own generic type.

In our code base, we have one util that is supposed to work with any type. It is a `Maybe` monad.

 If you have jumped to this chapter, then you may find it handy to read about monad patterns in `Chapter 9`, *Elements of Functional Programming Patterns*.

The `Maybe` monad is either `Nothing`, when the variable happens to be `null`, `undefined`, or `Something` of that type. This is a perfect fit for generic types:

```
export type MaybeType<T> = Something<T> | Nothing;

const Maybe = <T>(value: T):MaybeType<T> => {
    // ...
};
```

The tricky part is implementing `Something<T>` and `Nothing`. Let's start with `Nothing`, as it is much easier. It should return `null` on value check and always map to itself:

```
export type Nothing = {
    map: (args: any) => Nothing,
    isNothing: () => true,
    val: () => null
}
```

`Something<T>` should map to either `Something<MappingResult>` or `Nothing`. The value check should return `T`:

```
export type Something<T> = {
    map: <Z>(fn: ((a:T) => Z)) => MaybeType<Z>,
    isNothing: () => false,
    val: () => T
}
```

Mapping the result type is saved by using the `Z` generic type that is introduced in the `map` function signature.

However, if we try to use our newly defined types, they will not work. Unfortunately, TypeScript does not always figure out union types correctly. This problem occurs when union of types leads to different call signatures per specific key. In our case, this happens with the `map` function. Its type is `(args: any) => Nothing` or `<Z>(fn: ((a:T) => Z)) => MaybeType<Z>`. Hence, `map` has no compatible call signature.

The quick fix to this problem is defining a standalone `MaybeType` that satisfies two conflicting type definitions:

```
export type MaybeType<T> = {
    map: <Z>(fn: ((a:T) => Z)) => (MaybeType<Z> | Nothing),
    isNothing: () => boolean,
    val: () => (T | null)
}
```

With such a type definition, we can proceed to use the new generic type:

```
// src/ Chapter_11/
// Example_4/ src/ features/ tasks/ state/ selectors/ tasks.ts

export const tasksSelector =
    (state: TasksState):MaybeType<Immutable.Map<string, any>> =>
        Maybe<TasksState>(state).map((x:TasksState) => x.tasks);
```

The selector function takes `TasksState` as an argument and is expected to return a map that is assigned to the `tasks` key within the state. It may look a little tough to understand, hence, I highly recommend you to open the previous file and have a longer look. If you struggle, in the *Further reading* section at the end of the chapter, I have included a reference to an issue on GitHub that discusses this in detail.

Understanding TypeScript

In the previous section, we ran into a problem that is quite tough to understand if you have never worked with type systems. Let's learn a little bit about TypeScript itself to understand this better.

Type inference

The very first thing I want you to understand is type inference. You do not need to type everything. Some types can be inferred by TypeScript.

Imagine a situation where I have told you, "I have put only chocolate donuts in the box on your desk." Since, in this example, I pretend to be the computer, you can trust me. Hence, when you arrive at your desk, you are 100% sure that the box is of the `Box<ChocolateDonut[]>` type. You know this without opening the box or having an explicit sticker on it that says *Box full of chocolate donuts*.

In a real code, it works very similarly. Let's look at the following minimal example:

```
const someVar = 123; // someVar type is number
```

This is trivial. We can now look at something that I like more, `ChocolateDonuts`, as follows:

```
enum FLAVOURS {
    CHOCOLATE = 'Chocolate',
    VANILLA = 'Vanilla',
```

```
    }
    type ChocolateDonut = { flavour: FLAVOURS.CHOCOLATE }

    const clone = <T>(sth:T):T => JSON.parse(JSON.stringify(sth));

    const produceBox: <T>(recipe: T) => T[] = <T>(recipe: T) => [
        clone(recipe), clone(recipe), clone(recipe)
    ];

    // box type is inferred
    const box = produceBox<ChocolateDonut>({ flavour: flavours.CHOCOLATE });

    // inferred type correctly contains flavor key within donut object
    for (const donut of box) {
        console.log(donut.flavour);
    } // compiles and when run prints "Chocolate" three times
```

In this example, we exercise both the enum and generic types. The clone simply clones any type into a brand new one and delegates to JSON functions: stringify and then parse. The ProduceBox function simply takes a recipe and creates an array of clones based on that recipe. In the end, we create a box of chocolate donuts. The type is correctly inferred because we have specified a generic type for produceBox.

Structural typing

TypeScript uses structural typing. To understand what that means, let's look at the following example:

```
    interface Donut {
        flavour: FLAVOURS;
    }

    class ChocolateDonut {
        flavour: FLAVOURS.CHOCOLATE;
    }

    let p: Donut;

    // OK, because of structural typing
    p = new ChocolateDonut();
```

In this example, we first declare the p variable, and then assign a new instance of ChocolateDonut to it. It works in TypeScript. It wouldn't work in Java. Why?

We have never explicitly indicated that `ChocolateDonut` implements the `Donut` interface. If TypeScript did not use structural typing, you would need to refactor part of the preceding code to the following:

```
class ChocolateDonut implements Donut {
    flavour: FLAVOURS.CHOCOLATE;
}
```

The reasoning behind using structural typing is often referred as duck-typing:

> *If it walks like a duck and it quacks like a duck, then it must be a duck.*

Hence, `implements Donut` is not required in TypeScript, because `ChocolateDonut` already behaves like a donut, so it must be a donut. Hurray!

Immutability with TypeScript

In this section, I want to reiterate a point on immutability. This topic is huge in JavaScript, and in some cases, TypeScript may be a much better solution than any other path to immutability.

TypeScript comes with the special `readonly` keyword that enforces that a certain variable is read-only. You cannot mutate such a variable. This is enforced at compile time. Hence, you have no runtime checks for immutability. If this is a huge win for you, then you may not even need any API, such as Immutable.js. Immutable.js shines when you are required to clone huge objects to avoid mutations. If you can get away with a spread operation on your own, then it means your object may not be big enough for Immutable.js.

readonly

Since our application is not super big yet, as an exercise, let's replace Immutable.js with `readonly` from TypeScript:

```
export type TasksReducerState = {
    readonly entities: TaskType[],
    readonly isLoading: boolean,
    readonly hasError: boolean,
    readonly errorMsg: string
}
```

This looks like a lot of repetition. We can use Readonly< T > instead:

```
export type TasksReducerState = Readonly<{
    entities: TaskType[],
    isLoading: boolean,
    hasError: boolean,
    errorMsg: string
}>
```

This looks much cleaner. However, it is not entirely immutable. You can still mutate the entities array. To prevent that, we need to use ReadonlyArray<TaskType>:

```
export type TasksReducerState = Readonly<{
    entities: ReadonlyArray<TaskType>,
    // ...
}>
```

The remaining work is to replace every TaskType[] with ReadonlyArray<TaskType> throughout the entire application. Then you will need to change Immutable.js objects into standard JavaScript arrays. Such a refactor is long and does not fit in these book pages, but I have done the refactor in the code files. If you want to see what has changed, go to the code files directory at src/Chapter_11/Example_5.

Using linter to enforce immutability

You may use the TypeScript linter to enforce the readonly keyword in TypeScript files. One of the open source solutions that allows you to do this is tslint-immutable.

It adds additional rules to the tslint.json configuration file:

```
"no-var-keyword": true,
"no-let": true,
"no-object-mutation": true,
"no-delete": true,
"no-parameter-reassignment": true,
"readonly-keyword": true,
"readonly-array": true,
```

From now on, when you run linter, you will see errors if you violate any of the preceding rules. I have refactored the code to comply with them. Check the full example in code files directory at src/Chapter_11/Example_6. To run linter, you may use the following command in the Terminal:

```
yarn run lint
```

Summary

In this chapter, you have learned about a very powerful tool: typed language built on top of JavaScript. Type checking has countless advantages for any code base. It prevents you from deploying a breaking change that definitely does not comply with what is expected. You have learned how to tell TypeScript what is allowed. You know what generic types are, and how to use them to reduce code repetition in typed files.

New tools come with new knowledge, so you have also learned the basics of type inference and structural typing. This part of TypeScript definitely requires trial and error. Practice it to understand it better.

This is the last chapter of this book. I hope you have learned many interesting concepts and patterns. I have challenged you throughout this book; now it is time that you challenged your code base. See what fits your application and maybe rethink the choices you and your team made before.

Don't worry if you do not understand some patterns. Not all of them are a must. Some come with experience, some apply only to large code bases, and some are a matter of preference.

Choose the patterns that guarantee application correctness, as well as ones that enable you to add customer value more quickly. Good luck!

Further reading

- *Mastering TypeScript (Second edition)*, Nathan Rozentals: This is a great book to learn TypeScript in depth. It demonstrates how to type some really advanced use cases. This is my personal recommendation, not the publisher's.
- Official documentation for TypeScript can be found at `www.typescriptlang.org`.
- The discussion of the call signatures issue, mentioned previously in this chapter, can be found in the TypeScript GitHub repository at `https://github.com/Microsoft/TypeScript/issues/7294`.

Other Books You May Enjoy

If you enjoyed this book, you may be interested in these other books by Packt:

React and React Native - Second Edition
Adam Boduch

ISBN: 9781789346794

- Learn what has changed in React 16 and how you stand to benefit.
- Crafting reusable components using the React virtual DOM
- Using the React Native command-line tool to start new projects
- Augmenting React components with GraphQL for data using Relay
- Handling state for architectural patterns using Flux.
- Building an application for web UIs using Relay

React Cookbook
Carlos Santana Roldan

ISBN: 9781783980727

- Gain the ability to wield complex topics such as Webpack and server-side rendering
- Implement an API using Node.js, Firebase, and GraphQL
- Learn to maximize the performance of React applications
- Create a mobile application using React Native
- Deploy a React application on Digital Ocean
- Get to know the best practices when organizing and testing a large React application

Leave a review - let other readers know what you think

Please share your thoughts on this book with others by leaving a review on the site that you bought it from. If you purchased the book from Amazon, please leave us an honest review on this book's Amazon page. This is vital so that other potential readers can see and use your unbiased opinion to make purchasing decisions, we can understand what our customers think about our products, and our authors can see your feedback on the title that they have worked with Packt to create. It will only take a few minutes of your time, but is valuable to other potential customers, our authors, and Packt. Thank you!

Index

Printed in Great Britain
by Amazon